SICILY AND THE GREEKS

Maenad antefix from Morgantina, c. 550 B.C.

JEROME LECTURES   NINTH SERIES

Sicily and the Greeks

Studies in the Interrelationship
between the Indigenous Populations
and the Greek Colonists

Erik Sjöqvist

ANN ARBOR   THE UNIVERSITY OF MICHIGAN PRESS

To Richard Stillwell
with gratitude and affection

Preface

The excavations at Morgantina, conducted by the
Princeton University Expedition to Sicily beginning
in the summer of 1955, provided not only, as had been
hoped, the history of a site belonging to the
Hellenistic period in central Sicily, but much besides.

They furnished a very valuable body of material
that illuminated the Hellenic impact on the culture
of the island, and I have drawn extensively on this
factor in writing the Jerome Lectures contained in this
volume.

For its preparation I am especially indebted to
Mrs. E. Baldwin Smith for her help with the illustrations
and various amendments to the text, to Dr. Wathiq
Al-Salihi for valuable assistance with the footnotes, and
to Mr. Thor Robertsson, M.A., for compiling the
bibliography. Most of all I would acknowledge the
assistance of Richard Stillwell, my co-director in
the field.

ERIK SJÖQVIST

Contents

Illustrations

Abbreviations

Acta Inst. Rom. Suec.	*Skrifter utgivna av Svenska Institutet i Rom. Acta Instituti Romani Regni Sueciae*
AJA	*American Journal of Archaeology*
Annuario Scuola Atene	*Annuario della Scuola Archeologica di Atene e delle missioni italiani in Oriente*
Arch. Stor. Sic. Orient.	*Archivio Storico per la Sicilia Orientale*
Arch. St. Sir.	*Archivio Storico Siracusano*
Archeol. Class.	*Archeologia Classica*
BASOR	*Bulletin of the American Schools of Oriental Research in Jerusalem and Baghdad*
BCH	*Bulletin de Correspondance Hellénique*
Bd'A	*Bollettino d'Arte*
BEFAR	*Bibliothèque des Écoles Françaises d'Athènes et de Rome*
BPI	*Bullettino di Paletnologia Italiana*
BSA	*The Annual of the British School at Athens*
BSR	*Papers of the British School at Rome*
FHG	*Fragmenta Historicorum Graecorum* (ed. Müller)
Hesp.	*Hesperia. Journal of the American School of Classical Studies at Athens*
IG	*Inscriptiones Graecae*
Mon. Ant.	*Monumenti antichi pubblicati per cura della Reale Accademia Nazionale dei Lincei*
NSc.	*Atti della (–1946: Reale) Accademia (from 1921:) Nazionale dei Lincei. Notizie degli Scavi di Antichità*
Opusc. Rom.	*Opuscula Romana*
RE	*Pauly's Real-Encyclopädie der classischen Altertumswissenschaft*
Rend. Acc. Linc.	*Atti della (–1946: Reale) Accademia (from 1921:) Nazionale dei Lincei. Rendiconti*
Rev. Arch.	*Revue Archéologique*
Rhein. Mus.	*Rheinisches Museum für Philologie*
Röm. Mitt.	*Mitteilungen des Deutschen Archäologischen Instituts. Römische Abteilung*
SCE	*The Swedish Cyprus Expedition*
Studi Etr.	*Studi Etruschi*

1 *The Earliest Contacts between Greece and Sicily*

During the last fifteen years the learned literature on ancient Sicily has grown in a prodigious way. It is the effect of work by historians like E. Manni and his group in Palermo, by the late L. Pareti, by the British historian Woodhead, and by the German scholars such as Schenk von Staufenberg, Stroheker, Berve, and Wentker. The frontiers of our knowledge have been widened and advanced in an equally effective way by the work of archaeologists. Among them should, in first place, be mentioned L. Bernabò Brea and his able collaborators in the *Soprintendenza alle antichità* of Syracuse; D. Adamesteanu and P. Orlandini with their base of operations in Gela under the leadership of P. Grifo; the French scholars G. Vallet and F. Villard working at Megara Hyblaea, and V. Tusa, *soprintendente* in Palermo. The excavations and publications of these men and their colleagues contribute to the continuous growth of our study material. This material is thus increasing daily and, naturally, is in a fluid state.

It may, under these circumstances, seem a premature or even hazardous enterprise to attempt to circumscribe the problem and to discuss its various aspects under any form of synthesis.

To make such an attempt is not even my intention. In this series of lectures that carry the name of the late classicist and Italophile, Thomas Spencer Jerome, I intend only to gather and analyze the historical and archaeological material apt to illustrate the relationship between the indigenous populations of the island and the Greek colonists; to study the interdependence of these two ethnic elements, and to try to arrive at some conclusions bearing on the problem of when and how the great masses of indigenous inhabitants of central Sicily became Hellenized.

We know from ample evidence that they were completely Hellenized during the Hellenistic and Roman periods. Our interest is rather concentrated on the historical process which resulted in the Hellenization. Our attention will be directed toward the transformation itself. Simultaneously, the question will be asked whether and to what degree the Greek civilization of Sicily was conditioned or modified by the indigenous element.

A study of this kind cannot be initiated without mentioning the great scholars of the past generations. Paolo Orsi, Ettore Gabrici, Biagio Pace, and Thomas Dunbabin, who, with such indefatigable work and so much perspicacious learning, laid the foundations of our modern studies on ancient Sicily.

A study of the earliest contacts between Greece and Sicily carries us back in time to the Bronze Age of the second millennium B.C., a period which in the minds of the Greeks of historic times was immersed in heroic legends.

For the modern critic there exists a clear-cut border line between history and legend. The former is the reliable, orderly and controllable narration of the events of the past, while the latter is the fruit of creative and poetic imagination, using as motifs the fabulous enterprises of more or less imaginary heroes of the past.

Such a strict difference between history and legendary myth did not exist in the minds of the ancient Greeks. The myths were an integral part of their ancient history and were considered a material that could legitimately be used in actual political discussions and conclusions. It may suffice to recall that the historian, Diodorus Siculus, dedicated his first five books of his world history exclusively to myths and legends which to him represented the early history of the nations and the background necessary for the correct understanding and interpretation of subsequent events.

Few are the ancient historians who, like Thucydides (VI. 2.1–2) with so many words, separate "what has been said by the poets (ποιηταῖς εἴρεται) from what has been found to be the truth (ἀλήθεια εὑρίσκεται).

An archaeologist who works with historical problems of the heroic age is continuously confronted with literary sources of the legendary and mythological type. It is, therefore, his duty to take a clear position with regard to the value he thinks should be attributed to these sources in his toilsome task of reconstructing the past which has come down to us only in form of poor fragments of artifacts and as vague memories preserved in poetic legends.

The great quantity of mythographic material which has reached us through the ancient authors can, I believe, be conveniently subdivided into three distinct groups.

The first group contains the speculative myths created in order to explain the many natural phenomena which surrounded primitive man and to which he was unable to give a rational, or as we would say, a scientific explanation: the regular movements of the heavenly bodies, the rise and setting of the sun, the lightning and the thunder, the fertility of the soil and the growth cycle, not to mention the most mysterious of all natural secrets — the creation of the world and the beginning of things.

These are the speculative myths which are of an enormous interest to the intellectual and religious history of mankind, but which do not directly concern a historian or an archaeologist.

In the second group I would place the folktales of the traditional type: "Once upon a time . . ." They are the fruits of the free and purely poetic imagination innate in man. They recur in similar form in all countries from India to Iceland, and they describe in poetic form the fantastic adventures of witches and dwarfs, of beautiful princesses, courageous and noble young men who fight fabulous and dangerous monsters. They belong to the field of the literary historian and the folklorist. In them we meet the indomitable will of man trying to liberate himself from a dire reality and to flee to the green pastures of a fantastic and ideal world where nothing is impossible or improbable.

A third group is of special interest to us and that is the heroic legend. It deals with narrations of heroes or groups of heroes of the past with proper names and specific genealogies and with more or less precise geographic indications. The cycles of such legends are interconnected and interdependent and can follow the deeds of a family or a dynasty from generation to generation. They obtained their final form in later times, but were founded on a long oral tradition, sung by poets and bards through the centuries before entering literature in a fixed and final form.

During that long oral process they were transformed and modified. Details were suppressed or amplified. Motifs were added in order to serve better *ad maiorum gloriam.* Many elements of the folktale, always present in the poet's mind, invaded the narration as embellishments and could easily confuse it. The hard core of such a heroic legend can, however, very well contain a seed of truth because the oral tradition reaches right up to the heroic age itself, to the Bronze Age of the Aegean area.

Among these legendary cycles should be counted the *Iliad* and the *Odyssey,* the cycles of the Argonauts, of Heracles, of Theseus, and the epopees, now mostly lost, of the *Returns from Troy* (the *Nostoi*) and the *Destruction of Troy* (*Iliupersis*) and others.

It should be remembered that the historical importance attributed to the heroic legends in ancient times and the fact that they were often used as motivation or justification of political action in later historical periods frequently induced the mythographers to create a legend *ad hoc* to serve political aims. They could be used as arguments in territorial conflicts or as a stimulus of patriotic feelings in critical situations in the history of a people.

These "false" or aetiological legends are very numerous in ancient mythography and are, in themselves, not less interesting than the "genuine" ones. For the archaeologist and the historian whose task it is to reconstruct the distant past, they obviously possess a value very different from the original legend.

Which are the criteria for separating these two types of legends from one another? To be entitled to use a legend as a legitimate instrument, the historian and the archaeologist must be sure that its literary stemma is respectable and pure and that it antedates a given situation on which it could have served as a justification of political action.

We archaeologists are, however, not satisfied with the sole literary stemma of the legend. We require further proofs before accepting it as a valid element in the historical reconstruction of the past.

The additional proof should consist of external evidence, i.e., of archaeological finds. This, for understandable reasons, is an ideal which only rarely corresponds to actual reality.

Archaeological excavations are sporadic and the earth still hides much more than what the excavators have brought to light. The absence of archaeological confirmation of a legendary tradition can thus be of only temporary nature, and the lacuna can very well be filled by new discoveries from one day to another. A splendid example of such confirmation is found in Bernabò Brea's discovery of Apennine material in Lipari. It gives factual substance to the legend related by Diodorus Siculus (V. 7) of the colonization of the island by the legendary hero Liparus and his Italic Ausonians. Another example of less spectacular nature is furnished by the excavations being conducted by Princeton University at Morgantina. There the transition from Late Bronze to Early Iron Age is characterized by the appearance of ceramics of an equally Apennine *impasto* type. This surprising fact should be connected with the legend of Morges, the legendary founder of the town who, with his Morgetians, came to Sicily from south Italy.

Here are two examples of the rare and satisfactory

phenomenon when literary tradition and archaeological evidence seem to confirm each other and thus make valid the historical reconstruction. In both cases we deal with recent and completely unexpected discoveries.

On the other hand, it is needless to point out that an ample archaeological documentation needs no parallel legendary tradition to become a valid argument in the reconstruction of events of the past. Even without the passage in Diodorus Siculus, Bernabò Brea's discoveries would have justified the conclusion that toward the end of the Bronze Age Apennine immigrants colonized the island of Lipari.

It should also be remembered that the mythographic material which has come down to us from literary sources, abundant as it may seem, still is only a small fragment of the enormous treasure of stories, narrations, sagas, and myths which the ancient classical peoples had created, transformed, and embellished through the centuries. It is easy to remember that the archaeological material is fragmentary and fitful, but it is easier to forget that the literary legendary material is equally incomplete.

Keeping in mind these methodological considerations, we may proceed to examine some legends and test them by the critical criteria which are furnished in the fields of philology and archaeology.

The first legend is that dealing with Cocalus, the first king of the Sicans, and his relationship with King Minos of Crete and with Daedalus, as well as the arrival of Cretans in Sicily during prehistoric times.

The interpretation and historical evaluation of this legend have, in recent times, caused a lively discussion, in which the main participants are Dunbabin,[1] Bérard,[2] Pugliese Carratelli,[3] Becatti,[4] and Manni.[5] The two poles between which the discussion oscillates are clearly opposed to one another. On one side, one tries to vindicate the historicity of the myth and to consider it a "genuine" one, while, on the other side, the saga is considered an aetiological legend, invented in later times to serve political and ideological purposes during the period of the historical Greek colonization. Learned arguments have been mobilized on both sides *"et adhuc sub iudice lis est."*

We find the myth in its late and elaborate form in Diodorus Siculus (IV. 76–80). He begins his story with the enterprises of the Athenian master Daedalus who took refuge in Crete and entered into the service of King Minos of Knossos. There he built the famous Labyrinth. He had, however, to leave Crete precipitately when Minos discovered that he had assisted Pasiphaë in satisfying her monstrous passion for the bull by constructing the cow in which the queen concealed herself, later giving birth to the Minotaur. Daedalus escaped with his son, Icarus, flying over the sea, but the father alone, it will be remembered, reached safety in Sicily.

Up to this point, the story dwells in the realm of folktale and fantastic saga created by pure imagination. Such was also Diodorus's opinion, for he adds the phrase: "Although this story is completely incredible ($\pi\alpha\rho\acute{\alpha}\delta o\xi os$) we have decided not to leave it out of our narration."

Daedalus's goal was Sicily where he was received by Cocalus, king of the Sicans. There he remained for a long period of time. His admirable architectural talents were used and proved by Cocalus in various parts of the island. At Megara, on the east coast, he built a large reservoir for the River Alabo. Later, he built the city of Camicus in the region of the future city of Agrigentum. He fortified it so well that Cocalus chose the site for his capital. In the territory of Selinus he constructed a cave, heated by volcanic steam in such a way that it became useful for healing the sick.

At Eryx he built the great substructure of the temple of Aphrodite and many other monuments "which," says Diodorus, "have all been destroyed because of their great antiquity."

Here I would interrupt Diodorus for a moment and make a few factual remarks. Of the reservoir at Megara there are no traces, and the famous city of Camicus has not been found, in spite of intensive archaeological research carried out in the two regions. The remains of the terrace walls at Eryx are of a much later date and reveal no traces of earlier or prehistoric structures.

The fact that until this point of Diodorus's narration every archaeological confirmation of the story is missing should put us on guard against premature historical conclusions.

When Minos was informed that Daedalus was in Sicily, Diodorus continues, he organized a great naval expedition against the island. He landed in the neighborhood of Agrigentum in a place that was named Minoa after him. He asked of Cocalus that Daedalus should be delivered to him, and the Sican king listened to the request with simulated benevolence. First, however, he offered Minos a hot bath and suffocated him in the bath by raising the temperature too high. When he gave up the dead body to the Cretans, he made them believe that their king's death had been accidental. The Cretans built Minos a magnificent tomb, the upper part of which was a temple dedicated to Aphrodite, while the subterranean part served as a repository for the king's bones. Diodorus adds that the tomb remained substantially intact until the reign of Theron of Agrigentum in the early part of the fifth century B.C. He dismantled the building and sent the human remains of Minos back to Crete.

Some of the Cretans remained in Minoa while others, reinforced by a punitive expedition sent from Crete, moved toward the interior of the island where they founded the city of Engyon with its sanctuary dedicated to the mother goddesses.

Such is the substance of the legend as Diodorus Siculus tells it. Before attempting a historical evaluation of it, we have to submit it to the two critical tests: the literary and the archaeological.

From a literary point of view, parts of the story are found as early as in Herodotus (VII. 170) where we hear of Minos's death at Camicus and of the Cretan punitive expedition to Sicily. After having vainly besieged the city for five years, they had to leave the island. On their way home, they were overtaken by a storm and driven to the coasts of Apulia in the territory of the Japygians with whom the shipwrecked Cretans identified themselves. It should be noted that Herodotus, when relating this story, begins it with the word $\lambda\acute{\epsilon}\gamma\epsilon\tau\alpha\iota$, "it is told." By so doing, he disclaims any responsibility with regard to the veracity of the story. He knew, however, of the existence of the city of Camicus, $\tau\grave{\eta}\nu$ $\kappa\alpha\tau$ ' $\grave{\epsilon}\mu\grave{\epsilon}$ Ἀκραγαντῖνοι ἐνέμοντο, "occupied in my time by the Agrigentines." He further confirms that the naval expedition of the Cretans was undertaken on a large scale.

Other ancient traces of the legend are found in Strabo (VI. 2.6–7) who quotes the historian Antiochus of Syracuse, one of Herodotus's contemporaries. In principle, his story coincides with that of Herodotus, even with regard to the general reservation of $\lambda\acute{\epsilon}\gamma\epsilon\tau\alpha\iota$ with which he begins his narration.

We can thus follow the literary tradition to about the year 480 B.C. That means that it antedates Diodorus's narration by approximately four hundred years. The literary stemma is quite respectable and has to be taken seriously.

The differences between the Herodotean nucleus and Diodorus's story are, however, considerable. In the earlier version not only is the folktale motif of Minos's death in the bath missing, but also the story about the great Cretan conquests of the interior, the foundation of Engyon and — still more important — the foundation of the city of Minoa and the alleged tomb of Minos. The stories of Daedalus's works are also left out of the original version.

What the two versions have in common is the mention of Cocalus, king of the Sicans, his capital of Camicus, the Cretan expedition, and Minos's death in Sicily. If these parts of the legend have to be considered its hard core, it is not surprising that great scholars like Dunbabin and Manni consider "the Achaeo-Minoan episode in Sicily an established fact from a chronological and archaeological point of view."[6] Chronologically speaking, this episode should have taken place during the last quarter of the fifteenth century B.C. because it is tied to the collapse of Minoan power in Crete.

Before accepting such an interpretation, it is incumbent upon us to study the archaeological material which possibly could provide a concrete proof of a Minoan settlement in Sicily, or at least of such a strong Minoan influence that it could have motivated the legend.

Such a scrutiny brings about a completely negative result. Until now, nothing has been found in Sicily of purely Minoan material. The many and well-documented contacts between Sicily and the Aegean are manifest in the form of Mycenaean pottery found in various places on the island. Lord William Taylour,[7] who has studied the Aegean ceramics found in Italy and adjacent islands, registered only four genuinely Minoan fragments.[8] All of them were found in Lipari, a place which is in no way connected with the legend we have to examine.

The city of Minoa, later known as Heraclea-Minoa, has been excavated to a great extent by De Miro.[9] The excavations have brought to light not one single Minoan or Mycenaean fragment; they indicate, instead, that the town was a subcolony of Selinus founded in the second half of the sixth century B.C. A note to that effect is also found in Herodotus (V. 46). Add to this negative documentation the information found in Heraclides Ponticus that the town initially carried the Phoenician name Macara,[10] and the conclusion must be that the Minoan character of the town evaporates in a disconcerting way.

Camicus, Cocalus's capital, has not yet been found or

Fig. 1. Golden finger rings from S. Angelo Muxaro

identified. S. Angelo Muxaro in the valley of the Platani River north of Heraclea-Minoa was once considered the site of Camicus on the strength of the well-known gold objects found there.[11] The gold rings (Fig. 1) are, however, not Bronze Age imitations of Minoan originals but local products of the sixth or the beginning of the fifth century B.C.[12]

Dunbabin, who tended toward a positive interpretation of the legend, stressed in his discussion two particular circumstances.

The first of these is the so-called Temple-Tomb (Fig. 2) at Knossos, excavated by Sir Arthur Evans in 1931. Evans had naturally read Diodorus's description of the tomb of Minos with much interest and was eagerly looking forward to finding in Knossos a monument corresponding to the description. He thought that he had succeeded when he discovered the Temple-Tomb.[13] Giovanni Becatti has, however, clarified the problem. He has perspicaciously pointed out that the monument is neither a temple nor a tomb. In reality it is an elegant residence of the same type as the Royal Villa and the House of the Chancel Screen (Figs. 3, 4).[14] It was a rule among Minoan architects to make use of the sloping ground to create semi-subterranean space, very welcome refuges from the scorching heat of the Cretan summer. The Temple-Tomb shows no traces of an interment, and the room which Evans interpreted as a tomb chamber could be closed and locked by an intricate mechanism operable only from the inside of the room. Thus one of Dunbabin's main arguments in defense of the historicity of the legend is invalidated.

A second archaeological argument in favor of a

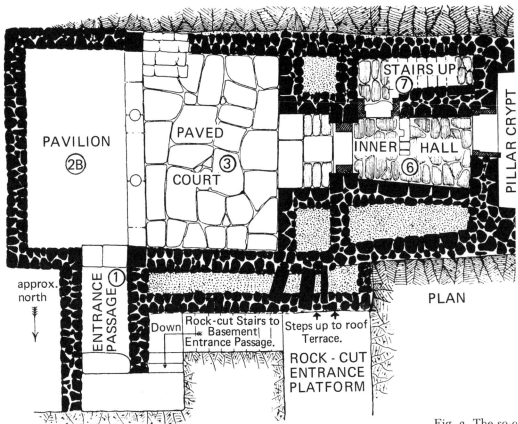

Fig. 2. The so-called Temple-Tomb at Knossos

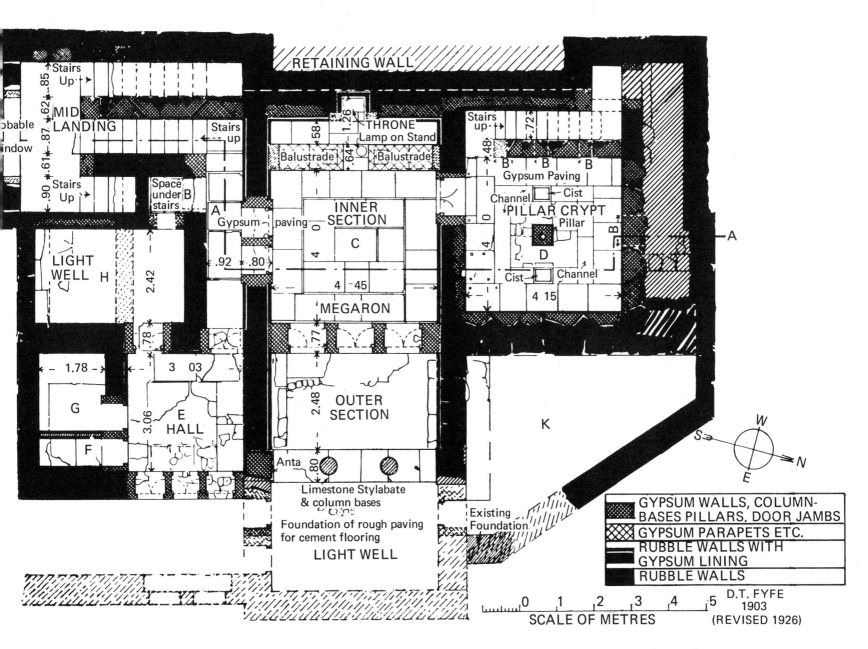

Fig. 3. The Royal Villa at Knossos

The Earliest Contacts 7

Fig. 4. The House of the Chancel Screen at Knossos

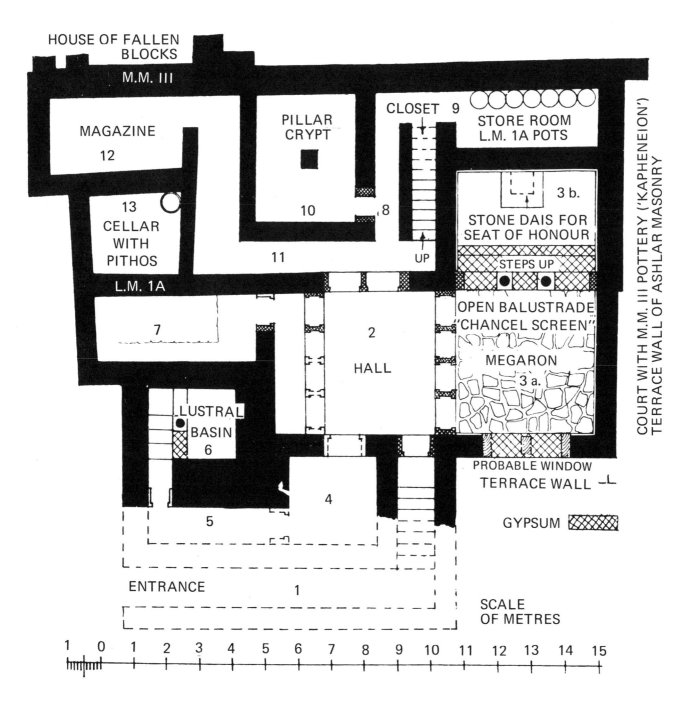

HOUSE OF FALLEN
BLOCKS

M.M. III

MAGAZINE
12

PILLAR
CRYPT

CLOSET 9

STORE ROOM
L.M. 1A POTS

13
CELLAR
WITH
PITHOS

10

8

3 b.

STONE DAIS FOR
SEAT OF HONOUR

11

STEPS UP

L.M. 1A

UP

7

2

HALL

OPEN BALUSTRADE
"CHANCEL SCREEN"

MEGARON
3 a.

LUSTRAL
BASIN
6

PROBABLE WINDOW

TERRACE WALL

4

GYPSUM

5

COURT WITH M.M. III POTTERY ('KAPHENEION')
TERRACE WALL OF ASHLAR MASONRY

ENTRANCE

1

SCALE
OF METRES

1 0 1 2 3 4 5 6 7 8 9 10 11 12 13 14 15

Cretan immigration to Sicily during the Bronze Age is quoted by Dunbabin. It deals with the presence of tholos tombs in Sicily during the fourteenth century B.C.

The argument is, in my opinion, not more convincing than the first, and that for two main reasons. First, the tholos tomb is not typical of Minoan civilization, but is rather a specific Mycenaean feature. Secondly, the so-called tholos tombs of Sicily are not situated in the Agrigentine region but along the east coast at Thapsos, Cozzo del Pantano and other neighboring sites.[15] Finally, these tombs have little or nothing in common even with the Mycenaean tholoi. They are low, rock-cut caves of modest dimensions. Their discoverer, Paolo Orsi, saw that this type of tomb was an offshoot of a long, local tradition of sepulchral architecture. He describes them correctly with these words: "They teach us nothing new. Their shape is that already known of a dome. I noticed some attempts which convey the idea of a low circular tent or a primitive hut."[16]

Under these circumstances they can in no way render substance to the presumed Minoan colonization indicated by the legend of Cocalus and Minos.

What should, then, be our conclusions with regard to the legend? Two ways lie open.

The first leads to a negation of every historical value of the legend because the assumed archaeological proofs of its being genuine are false, insufficient, or even contradictory. The legend would thus be of a purely aetiological character, created in a much later period to serve as a pseudo-historic justification of political and territorial claims of the historic epoch. Such an epoch would obviously coincide with the historical colonization of Gela and Agrigentum by Cretans and Rhodians of the seventh and sixth centuries B.C. and their subsequent conquest of the hinterland. Such is the position of Freeman,[17] Pais,[18] and Pareti.[19]

The place name of Minoa should have served as a starting point for the mythographer. It is a rather common toponym in the Aegean area, and could, in this case, have been invented and propagated by the Cretans of Gela and Agrigentum in order to justify their expansion policy and their conquests. We will learn, in due course, that their drive in such a direction was decisive and hard (see pp. 39–43).

The fact that the legendary enterprise of Minos ended so ignominiously could have given to the historic conquest of the interior by the Cretans a tint of justified revenge.

Against such a negative and radical solution speaks the literary stemma of the legend, traces of which go to Herodotus and Antiochus of Syracuse, i.e., to the first quarter of the fifth century B.C.

A second possibility involves a double attitude. One should first peel off the legend, as it were, all of its later Diodorean additions which lack counterparts in the earlier tradition and then interpret the rest in a less specific way. In Diodorus alone we find the tale of the foundation of Minoa, the Cretan conquest of the interior, and the foundation of Engyon. This could all very well be an aetiological addition created in historical times for reasons already mentioned.

The rest of the legend, interpreted in a general fashion, would leave intact the figure of King Cocalus, who is probably invested with a certain historicity. His contacts with the Minoan world should reflect not a specific bond between Crete and Sicily but only contacts between the Mycenaean-Aegean world and the island. During the times of the last King Minos, Crete had been in fact Achaean for two centuries. Daedalus was not a Cretan but an Athenian.

The place name of the city of Minoa became the crystallizing point for the fatal introduction of Minos in the legendary story. It cannot be excluded that the toponymic confusion was introduced on purpose to serve the ambitions of the Geloans and the Cretans in historic times. This does not mean that the name was simply invented. The story is probably more complicated than that. As has already been pointed out, Heraclea-Minoa was a subcolony of Selinus. The Sicilian metropolis of Selinus was Megara Hyblaea, itself a colony of Megara in Greece. In the territory of the Greek Megara there existed a place called Nisaea Minoa.[20] The name was thus in all probability originally Megarian and was later used by the Cretans of Gela and Agrigentum in order to substantiate their legendary Sicilian history. This would then have been the last aetiological manipulation, based on the equivocal place name, perpetrated by the Agrigentines *ad maiorum gloriam.*

All this is possible, even probable; but it certainly cannot be proved. From a methodological point of view, the question must be left open with this indication only of a solution acceptable to the historian and — with some

Fig. 5. Mycenaean III A three-handled jar from Agrigentum

reservations — also to the archaeologist.

In Agrigentum itself, the epicenter of the legend, there exist safe traces of contacts with the Mycenaean world. A small three-handled jar (Fig. 5) of the type Mycenaean III A from the fourteenth century B.C. was found in Agrigentum itself and gives us the positive proof of such contacts.

Close to Agrigentum, at Caldare, a tomb was excavated containing among other finds two bronze basins and two knife blades,[21] all of which very easily could have been direct imports from Mycenaean Greece.

The archaeological harvest is rather meager, especially considering that this part of the south coast has been the object of intensive investigation. It is also strange that Gela itself, the original center of the Cretans and the Rhodians, has not yielded a scrap of Mycenaean material.

In striking contrast to this paucity of archaeological finds is the wealth of Mycenaean ceramics in the region around Syracuse on the east coast (Figs. 6a, 6b). There it

Fig. 6a. Mycenaean vases from the neighborhood of Syracuse

Fig. 6b. Mycenaean vase from the neighborhood of Syracuse

The Earliest Contacts 11

Fig. 7. Mycenaean III B shards from Morgantina

abounds in places like Thapsos, Matrensa, Floridia, Cozzo del Pantano and Molinello.[22]

This zone lies beyond the sphere of influence of the legend of Cocalus and Minos and is only tangentially connected with the activities of Daedalus at Megara. Instead, it is intimately connected with the legendary cycle of Heracles and with his arrival in Sicily.

This legend, also to be found in Diodorus (IV. 22–24), has already been treated by this author in another publication.[23] It is thus unnecessary to repeat it here. May it suffice to say that its literary stemma can be followed up to Stesichorus in the first half of the sixth century B.C., and that M. P. Nilsson's thesis on the Mycenaean origin of the cycle of Heracles' labors[24] has to be accepted in principle. We are on much firmer philological ground than was the case with the Cocalus-Minos legend.

Heracles' tenth labor, the capture of the cattle of Geryon, brought him to Italy and Sicily. We may, for our present purposes, leave out the first part of the tale which deals with his conquest of the territory of Eryx and his subsequent return to the indigenous population. We shall turn, instead, to his activities in the region "where today the city of Syracuse is located." (IV. 23.4–5).

We meet him in his usual capacity as the civilizer of barbarian lands. He instituted the cult of Persephone at the spring of Cyane and then turned with his flock to the interior of the island. There the Sicans opposed his march with great forces. "Heracles conquered them," says Diodorus, "in a splendid battle and killed many, among whom, it is said, there were many illustrious chieftains as Leucaspis, Pediocrates, Bouphonas, Glychatas, Bytaeas, and Crytidas. After this, he crossed the plain of Leontini and admired its beauty and left with the inhabitants immortal remembrances of his presence."

The end of the Diodorean narration tells us that he received divine honors in Agyrium, Diodorus's native town, and that he thereafter left Sicily for Italy.

The myth presents Heracles' activities in Sicily, both in Eryx and in the interior of the island, as short raids not followed by any permanent conquest. In that sense they are profoundly different from those of Minos and the Cretans. We have to deal with quick advances followed by splendid victories—and immediate retreats. In mytho-logical form they do not reflect anything but temporary contacts. Syracuse was his base of operations, and it is precisely in that region that the mass of the Mycenaean ceramic material has been found.

The Sican heroes with whom he fights carry strange names. They are Greek in form, but they are not real proper names, only appellative denominations never carried by true Greeks. Leucaspis, Pediocrates and Bouphonas are descriptive in character: "The man with the white shield," "The ruler of the plain," and "The killer of bulls." The significance of the other names is less clear, but all seem to be brief Greek descriptions of anonymous barbarians.[25]

Heracles' raids into the interior were of short duration and of little consequence. Nonetheless, they can still be traced in archaeological finds which, in that sense, tend to confirm the legend. At Buscemi, approximately fifty kilometers from Syracuse, has been found a stirrup vase, still unpublished, of Mycenaean III B type from the thirteenth century B.C.[26] At the very center of the island, on the acropolis of Morgantina, Mycenaean shards (Fig. 7) of the same period came to light in 1959.[27] The exploration of central Sicily is still very sporadic, and the future may yield a fuller documentation, but I feel that I am already able to suggest some conclusion.

The first contacts between the Aegean world and Sicily proper were not of a penetrating or permanent character. There were no migrations or conquests on a big scale, as one could be induced to believe by the myth of Cocalus and Minos. Reduced to its original nucleus also, this legend coincides substantially with the more reliable one of Heracles. We have to count with a more or less permanent base, probably in the form of an emporium in Syracuse, and possibly of another in the region of Agrigentum. From them radiated the commercial contacts with the indigenous populations of the interior. In addition, these modest contacts document the relative unity of the Mediterranean world in which Sicily became included in the second millennium B.C. They also prove the civilizing force which emanated from the Aegean centers to Sicily as a precursor of later historical events.

On that score, legend and archaeology are in full agreement.

2 The Historic Greek Colonization: History and Archaeology

The contacts between Sicily and the Mycenaean world may be difficult to define and sometimes hard to trace in the maze of legend and in the sporadic archaeological material. This much can, however, be safely said: that these contacts existed and that they were of a seemingly casual and tangential character.

In Sicily proper we have no signs of any permanent colonial installation. The region of Syracuse, Heracles' legendary base of operations, may have served as a temporary trading station. More than that cannot be deduced from available evidence. On the Lipari Islands there may have been a more substantial and permanent installation, but again, most probably based on trade, not colonization and territorial domination.

What sort of goods were traded? It is not difficult to imagine what the Mycenaeans brought with them: artifacts and ready made goods of every kind: vases, bronze weapons and utensils (a sword found at Plemmyrion is probably of Mycenaean manufacture;[1] and two bronze cauldrons from Caldare may possibly have the same origin),[2] simple ornaments such as beads and necklaces of glass paste (also recorded in Sicily),[3] and other things that a sophisticated civilization could offer an underdeveloped area.

But what could they bring back from Sicily that Greece proper did not already possess? The obsidian from Lipari must have been a staple item in early times, but what did Sicily itself contribute? It might conceivably have been bulk goods as grain, leather, wine, and honey for which the island was rightly famous from early historical times, and possibly also slaves and prisoners.

These questions cannot be answered, but it should be remembered that trade required two things: 1) relative safety on the seas, and 2) a well organized and categorized society. Both were at hand in Mycenaean times.

When in the twelfth century B.C. the raids of "the peoples of the North and of the Islands of the Seas" broke up the relative unity of the Mediterranean world and when Mycenae and the Greek mainland were overrun by what we call the Dorian migrations, the Western outposts of the Mycenaean sphere of interest lost the very base of their existence. They were swallowed up and merged in an indigenous κοινή which shows only very rare instances of a continuation in the Aegean tradition.

Thucydides (VI. 2.4–5) tells us that this was the time when the Sicels passed over the straits from Italy to

14

Sicily and occupied the better part of the island, driving the aboriginal Sicans back to the western parts of Sicily, "and the Sicels still inhabit the central and northern regions." These events took place "nearly three hundred years before the arrival of the Hellenes," as Thucydides says, which in our chronology would mean the middle of the eleventh century B.C.

Archaeology can in some precious instances verify the Thucydidean story, but that is a chapter which is out of context in a study of Sicily and the Greeks.

The next installment in Thucydides' story is not directly connected with our topic either, but it has to be briefly discussed because of the general interest it attracts in the main discussion of early Sicilian history.

This is what Thucydides says (VI. 2.6): "The Phoenicians at one time had settlements (ᾤκουν) all around the island. They fortified promontories on the sea coast and settled in the small islands adjacent, for the sake of trading with the Sicels (ἐμπορίας ἕνεκα). But when the Greeks began to find their way by sea to Sicily in greater numbers they withdrew from the larger part of the island, and forming a union, established themselves in Motya, Soloeis and Panormus, in the neighbourhood of the Elymians, partly trusting to their alliance with them, and partly because this is the point at which the passage from Carthage to Sicily is shortest."

Thucydides is here very explicit, and it is only with the greatest hesitation that one questions the veracity of his statements.[4] There is little doubt that the Phoenicians of Tyre were trading with the West long before the Greek colonists landed in Sicily. We have them presumably on the Atlantic coast of Spain at Gades in the tenth century B.C. and in Utica in present-day Tunisia possibly in the early ninth century B.C.[5] A network of far-flung commercial routes needed landing stations and emergency harbors, but did they really need all the promontories, islets and harbors all around Sicily as permanent installations and ports of call? And, if that were the case, did the Phoenicians without any resistance give up these priceless holdings on the arrival of the Greeks, abandoning control of the Strait of Messina and the rich east and south coasts and contenting themselves with the much less wealthy and attractive northwest corner of the island? Such a procedure would seem particularly difficult to understand, if they had their powerful mother city, Carthage, within easy reach on the African coast.

The question is asked not only for rationalistic reasons, but also, above all, because there are no archaeological traces of their assumed fortifications and installations anywhere on the east coast where the Greeks first landed, and these sites have for long been the objects of intensive archaeological exploration. Nor are any finds recorded of Punic pottery or other artifacts in these areas. Irrefutable evidence of the intermittent presence of the Phoenicians in the West, if not in Sicily, do however exist. There is the Phoenician inscription from Nora in Sardinia, dated by Albright to the ninth century B.C.[6] and a small statuette of the Phoenician god Melqart, recently found by fishermen off the south shore of Sicily.[7]

A fragment of the Greek historian Timaeus tells us that Carthage, Καρχεδών, was founded by Pygmalion thirty-eight years before the first Olympic games, which in our chronology means a foundation date of 814 B.C. This tradition is taken for granted and accepted by most scholars and by all handbooks[8] without further discussion, but the problem is more complicated.

Carthage, in Phoenician — Quart-hadasht — means "the new capital city," and Phoenician history knows of two "new capitals" founded in different periods and on different sites. They were the capital of the vassal kingdom of Kition in Cyprus, and the city of Cathage itself.

The Greek form Pygmalion corresponds to the Cypriot-Phoenician Pumiathon, a dynastic name in Kition,[9] while in Carthage the common royal name is Ba'alu, the Belus of the *Aeneid*.

The Swedish excavations in Cyprus have traced the foundation of Kition to about 800 B.C.[10] while the French archaeologist Cintas has systematically searched the cemeteries of Carthage without finding anything earlier than the first quarter of the seventh century.[11]

All this is barely indicative, but it becomes meaningful in the light of other external evidence provided by Assyrian historical sources recently interpreted by Emil Forrer.[12] He deduced from Assyrian texts and historical records that the foundation of the second Phoenician "new capital," the real and historical Carthage, took place about 673 B.C., a period of great distress in the history of Tyre, the Phoenician mother city in Syria. Then it was threatened and blocked by Esarhaddon of Assyria, and part of the population under the leadership of Ba'alu and his daughters, Anna and Dido, made their way out of the blockade to found the Quart-Hadasht. We cannot help recognizing the Belus and Dido of the *Aeneid*. This would explicitly and implicitly suit the new situation. It was only when the "*old* capital" Tyre fell under the yoke of Assyria that the "*new* capital" Carthage was founded.

Forrer was unaware of, or at least uninterested in, the consequences his interpretation carried for Greco-Punic history in the West, nor did he seem to know of the implicit confirmation Cypriote, Sicilian, and Punic archaeology provide to his hypothesis. All the evidence taken together, however, makes his conclusion very attractive, as has been clearly pointed out by the French archaeologist Frézouls.[13]

If Carthage did not exist as a Punic stronghold at the arrival of the Greek colonists, we can better understand the behavior of the Phoenician tradesmen along the shores of Sicily. Their scattered, temporary emporia were not permanently fortified installations, and they had to yield to the forceful Greek mass colonization, leaving no material traces behind.

It was only after the foundation of Carthage that they came back in force, but then they had to be content with the region that the Greeks had left untouched: the rather poor northwest corner of the island where they planted their three cities of Motya, Panormus, and Soloeis.

This interpretation of historical and archaeological arguments modifies to some extent the narration of Thucydides, but does not touch the essential core of the study, i.e., that Phoenician tradesmen and explorers knew of the western trade routes before the Greek colonists set out westward.

The Greeks of the eighth century B.C. were well acquainted with the astute seafaring Phoenician tradesmen. We can read of them in the *Odyssey* in Odysseus's imaginary story told to Eumaeus (XIV. 288: φοῖνιξ ἦλθεν ἀνήρ) and in Eumaeus's own tale of the adventures of his childhood (XV. 415 ff.).[14]

The Greeks learned much from them. The Phoenicians gave them the acrophonetic alphabet and probably the calendar, and introduced them to the arts of the Near East. They were the explorers of the West, of which an East Ionian Greek like Homer knew nothing but the fantastic tales of Cyclops, Laestrygonians, Circe, Scylla, Charybdis, and the Sirens.

The Phoenicians' great importance to the historic development of the West rests in the fact that they were the precursors of the Greeks and led the way as explorers and tradesmen, not as settlers and colonists. In that sense, Thucydides is doubtless correct when giving to the Phoenicians the priority over the Greeks in this area. It was in the wake of the Phoenician commercial ships that the Greeks came to Sicily and Magna Graecia. The memories of their own historic past in the Mycenaean period were long since faded, and the colonization was a fresh start from scratch. Strabo is right when he asserts (VI. 2.2 /267/), "Before that time men were so afraid of the bands of pirates and the savagery of the barbarians in this region that they would not so much as sail thither for trafficking (καὶ ἐμπορίαν πλεῖν)." This is in sober prose the same story as that reflected in the *Odyssey* where Eumaeus was kidnapped by Phoenician raiders and where the folktales of Polyphemus, Scylla, and the Sirens flourished.

Very soon this lack of precise information on the western world was to be filled by the first historical colonists.

Thucydides, in his *locus classicus* (VI. 3–5), tells us very factually the sequence of events. I quote the beginning of the story:

"The first Greek colonists sailed from Chalcis in Euboea under the leadership of Thucles and founded Naxos; there they erected an altar to honor Apollo, The Leader, which is still standing outside the town, and on this altar religious embassies sacrifice before they sail from Sicily." This, then, is the beginning of a new chapter in the history of Sicily, and the altar of Apollo stood as an eternal guarantee of the priority of the Chalcidian Naxos over all the other Greek colonies in Sicily.

Thucydides then proceeds in chronological order and tells us that the year after Naxos, Syracuse was founded by the Corinthians under Archias. Five years later the Naxians founded Leontini and Catane. The stream of colonists was rapidly gaining momentum.

Next in order comes Megara Hyblaea, but there something of the clarity and precision of Thucydides seems to be lacking.[15] He uses the phrase κατὰ δὲ τὸν αὐτὸν χρόνον, "about the same time," and tells us of the vagaries of the Megarians before finally settling in Megara Hyblaea: ὕστερον and ὀλίγον χρόνον, "later" and "a little time" are the adverbs he uses, and we remain puzzled by the vagueness of the account. But once settled, the Megar-

Fig. 8. Early shards from Megara Hyblaea

Fig. 9. Early vase from Naxos

ians remained in their city for 245 years, and they were then driven out by Gelon of Syracuse.

This information gives us one key to the Thucydidean chronology, because we know that Gelon conquered Megara Hyblaea in the year 483 B.C. The rest is simple addition and subtraction: 483 and 245 make 728, which places Megara's foundation in the year 728 B.C. That should be "about the same time" as Catane and Leontini were founded by the Naxians, five years after Syracuse, founded in 733 B.C., and six years after Naxos, the foundation date of which should thus be 734 B.C.

These dates are of enormous importance not only to the history of Sicily, but also, indirectly, to Greece proper, as they become the cornerstones of the chronology of proto-Corinthian and Corinthian pottery which plays an important rôle in dating Greek archaic sites. They are generally accepted as a much-needed fixed point, but they have not remained entirely unchallenged, and there are some good reasons for this.

Thucydides' source was Syracusan and, therefore, possibly biased in favor of Syracuse. In his sequence it becomes the first Doric colony in Sicily and comes only one year after the incontestable Naxos. Conflicting evi-

dence is brought in by Diodorus Siculus (XIII. 59) whose main sources were Timaeus and Ephorus. In his calculations, based on homeland Greek sources, the foundation of Megara would be brought up in time to the year 751 and thus antedate Syracuse. Naxos would then have been founded six years earlier, i.e., 757 B.C.[16] The difference is twenty-three years and may rightly not seem too important, particularly as it does not affect the foundation date of Syracuse, which may remain fixed at the year 733 B.C. However, the foundation dates of Megara Hyblaea and the Chalcidian colonies of Naxos, Catane, and Leontini may be pushed twenty-three years further back. It is, of course, very difficult to apply archaeological criteria for the confirmation of one or the other date, but the two French scholars who are excavating Megara Hyblaea, Vallet and Villard, seem to me to be right when they maintain that the earliest proto-Corinthian Geometric pottery from Megara (Fig. 8) looks stylistically earlier than its counterparts from Syracuse.[17] These shards should be compared with what has recently been found at Naxos,[18] the undisputed nestor of the Sicilian colonies (Fig. 9). They are precisely of the same type as those of Megara, and they would thus confirm the high date of this site. That suggests, by inference, that the higher chronology for Naxos of 757 B.C. is indirectly confirmed.

A literary support for this date is provided by an independent tradition going back to Ephorus, the fourth-century Ionian historian, quoted by Strabo (VI. 2.2/267/), who tells us that Naxos and Megara were the first cities which the Greeks founded in Sicily. The same information meets us in Pseudo-Scymnos (V. 276 f.), testifying to the strength of the tradition.

The conflict between Thucydides and his Syracusan source on one side and the Ephorus-Timaeus-Diodorus-Strabo version on the other is a real one, and it cannot be solved by any compromise. The dilemma remains but can perhaps be explained. I would like to offer the following comments.

It is generally admitted that Thucydides, who must have visited Syracuse to judge from his precise and detailed knowledge of Syracusan topography, drew the information on the early history of the colonies from Syracusan sources, which means his early contemporary, Antiochus of Syracuse, and local archives.

The main sources of Diodorus were Ephorus and Timaeus of Tauromenium who lived his life in exile in Athens, studying Greek archives so zealously that Polybius (XII. 23–28) calls him an impractical and despicable historian. Diodorus's information is thus based on Greek, non-Sicilian source material. The same holds true for the Ionian, Ephorus.

Would it not have been a natural, if not excusable, tendency in mighty Syracuse to press its own priority a little above the limit allowed by factual history, and so to give to its own fifth century hegemony and early history a luster which it really lacked? Should Megara Hyblaea, brutally destroyed by the Syracusan tyrant Gelon in 483 B.C., be left with a better claim on the Syracusan territory than Syracuse herself? A slight "adjustment" of the tradition would take care of the situation, and I am inclined to believe in a local Syracusan falsification politically motivated, swallowed by Antiochus, and passed on to Thucydides. This would explain the studiously vague phraseology used in the story of the foundation of Megara which was preceded by movements from one place to another before the settlement was established. No specific time or year is given for the event, and Thucydides uses the phrase κατὰ δὲ τὸν αὐτὸν χρόνον, "about the same time."

Naxos could not be dislocated from its historic priority because there stood still the altar of Apollo Archegetes, the initiator of the colonization. It retained its indisputable place at the top of the list, but it was made to precede the foundation of Syracuse by barely one year.

The final result would then be that in the Syracusan tradition, followed by Thucydides, Naxos and Megara received lower foundation dates than they actually had, while Syracuse's own date is correctly given.

This higher chronology does not carry with it a revision of the whole list of foundation dates for the rest of the Sicilian colonies, and it certainly has no impact on Syracuse's own secondary colonies of Acrae, Casmenae, and Camarina. It must, however, involve Catane and Leontini, because they are tied to the year of the foundation of Megara.

Assuming then that the Ephorus-Timaeus tradition for Megara Hyblaea is right, we get the year 751 B.C. as its foundation date. Naxos preceded Megara by six years and would thus be tentatively brought to 757 B.C., while Catane and Leontini have to be placed at an uncertain date between 757 and 751 B.C.

Syracuse retains its date of 733 B.C. and becomes number five in line of priority among the Sicilian colonies instead of number two, preceded by the three Chalcidian Ionian cities of Naxos, Catane, and Leontini, and — what was possibly more painful — losing the priority among the Dorians to Megara Hyblaea.

Apollo Archegetes, the Supreme Leader, had his cult place in Naxos and was revered by all the Sicilian Greeks. The reason for this is to be found in the special procedure followed when the foundation of a new colonial city was decided by the Greeks of Hellas.

Our information on such matters is not very abundant, but what we have comes from respectable sources. Herodotus (V. 42) tells us of the events after Cleomenes I had become king of Sparta in 519 B.C., much to the dismay of his half-brother, Dorieus. The latter, in his indignation, "asked the Spartans for a body of men and took them off to found a colony (ἀποικία) elsewhere, without previously consulting the Delphic oracle or observing any of the usual formalities (τὰ νομιζόμενα). . . . Angry as he was, he directed the ships to Libya."

His was an ill-fated expedition, and it is to be understood that the reason for his lack of success was his negligence toward Delphi and τὰ νομιζόμενα. To these customary formalities belonged obviously a consultation of the Delphic oracle which authorized the enterprise so that it automatically received the protection of Apollo Archegetes.[19] It would have been gratifying if Herodotus had told us some more about what Dorieus dispensed with before the start of his hapless expedition, but he does not. Nor does Cicero when he exclaims (*De div.* I. i. 3): "What colony did Greece ever send out without consulting Delphi's, Dodona's, or Ammon's oracles?"[20] If Aristotle's work Περὶ ἀποίκων (On Colonists) had survived, we would certainly have known considerably more, but now we have to piece together our knowledge from many different and sometimes unclear indications in ancient texts.

Our first conclusion is that a colony foundation was a sacred state act where the Delphic oracle played a preponderant rôle. As the colonists always set out overseas, it is quite natural that Poseidon should also become involved. This happened especially in Corinth where he long since had enjoyed a particularly favored position among the state cults.

Another ritual and ceremonial bond between the emigrants and those who stayed at home was the usage of carrying on the long journey fire from the state hearth in the prytaneion of the mother city and using it for lighting the prytaneion fire of the colony.

The colonists, the ἄποικοι (literally "those separated from home"), received at the outset an οἰκιστής (a leader or founder). He could be elected by the departing colonists and, in such cases, seems to have been the leader of the political opposition at home, as was Dorieus, and before him the Partheniae who colonized Tarentum, also from Sparta. If the reason for the colonial enterprise was not political or ideological, but demographic and economic, he was nominated and elected by the regular political apparatus of the mother city. This is, I presume, what Plato favors when the new and ideal state should be founded (*Laws*, 4.708 B): "Now, colonization does not become easy if it does not take place like the departure of a swarm of bees (τὸν τῶν ἐσμῶν τρόπον), one group going as a friend among friends, pressed by the lack of land (στενοχορίᾳ γῆς) or necessitated by some other similar hardship (τίσιν ἄλλοις τοιούτοις παθήμασιν)."

In addition, the οἰκιστής had to promulgate a constitution, a πολιτεία. It seems to have been the rule that the new constitution was rather closely copied on that of the metropolis. The founder had also to lead the colonists in the planning of the new city and to attend to the delicate task of dividing the new land among the settlers. He certainly remained on the political scene as a leading figure as long as he lived, obtained in some cases the right to be buried within the city walls and finally often received offerings as a hero after his death.

The later part of the eighth century B.C. was the period of oligarchic aristocratic rule in Greece, and it is thus only natural that the new Sicilian colonies started their lives in the same political climate.

Such is the case story for a regular colony, an ἀποικία, and the result was an independent and sovereign political unit, the members of which renounced their old citizenships and became fully privileged citizens of the new colony.

The passages quoted from Herodotus and Plato indicate two of the main reasons for the foundation of colonies. One is political and ideological conflict at home, and the other is "the lack of land or other similar hardship." The latter was probably the more compelling and common situation. The pinch of the population explosion in a rapidly expanding archaic Greek society made emigration and colonization mandatory because Greek territory was limited, its valleys narrow and its plains small. It is hunger for land and for new and better possibilities of sustaining a growing population that was the most important factor promoting the Greek colonization. We can indirectly see this circumstance reflected in the name the original settlers of Syracuse adopted as a social distinction: γαμόροι, "owners of land."

Trade and commercial interests may have played their part also, but, in general, they followed in the wake of the colonists who had left home primarily for demographic and agricultural reasons.

The public and sacred ceremonies which preceded the foundation of a colony tied it with special bonds to Apollo and to Delphi. This circumstance may be of some importance for our judgment of the reliability of mainland Greek sources concerning the chronology of the colonies themselves. The sacred calendar was under the control and protection of this pan-Hellenic sanctuary, and from the year of the first Olympiad, i.e., 776 B.C., we seem entitled to consider it a source of reliable information. One would like to think that the oracular archives kept some record of such important events as foundations of colonies, and that they may have served the historians of the fifth century B.C. If this was the case, greater credence should be granted the chronological data which have just been discussed.

So much for the original establishment of the Greek colonies on the east coast of Sicily, the arrival of the ἄποικοι. We meet, however, another term sometimes wrongly considered a synonymous word for ἄποικοι, and that is ἔποικοι. The ἔποικοι were also colonists, but they did not automatically have the same rights as the original ἄποικοι. They were latecomers who, attracted by the gleaming tales from the new western world, joined an already established colony. They may have come from the old metropolis or from elsewhere and were accepted on conditions, varying from case to case and not excluding even equal rights with the original settlers. But it is clear that the founders gave up nothing of their land to the newcomers, and it is equally clear that the former had already the best land in firm personal possession. The ἔποικοι, therefore, often created a city-dwelling, middle class depending for their sustenance on their own skill, talents and resources. They were artisans, industrialists, merchants, the rank and file of the army — ὁ δῆμος — and they became the core of that bourgeois group on which many "tyrants" of the Sicilian cities based their power.

What is more important for our purposes is that they also became the driving force toward new colonization further inland, the avant garde of the penetration of central Sicily and the Hellenizers of the interior.

3 The Chalcidian Colonies of the East Coast and Their Penetration of the Hinterland

The Greek colonies of the east coast were soon solidly entrenched in their new territories and grew quickly in wealth and population (πολυάνθρωπος ἐγένετο, as Thucydides says about Syracuse, VI. 3). The Sicels seem to have put up very weak and scattered resistance against the landing Greeks, and we know only little about their first contacts. In the case of Megara, a Sicel chieftain called Hyblon even guided the Greeks and handed the place over to them voluntarily. These particularly peaceful relations seem reflected in the name of the new city, Megara Hyblaea, a combination of Greek and Sicel elements. In other cases, the newcomers had to fight their way in, as was the situation, for example, in Syracuse (Thuc. *ibid.*).

In front of the Greeks in the two new cities of Catane and Leontini lay the wide and fertile plains of the immediate hinterland which still constitute the most productive agricultural area of the island. There was the new land that the colonists had dreamed of and which the Sicels had held for three hundred years, πρὶν Ἕλληνες ἐς Σικελίαν ἐλθεῖν (Thuc. VI. 2). Neither from Thucydides nor from any other ancient source do we obtain any information on how the Greek takeover of this valuable land took place. The only indication we have is in Thucydides (*ibid.*) where we learn that after the arrival of the Greeks the Sicels withdrew to the interior and northern parts of the island where they still lived in his days (ἔτι δὲ καὶ νῦν . . . ἔχουσιν). This seems to indicate that the plain was soon incorporated into the territory (χῶρα) of the new Chalcidian colonies and probably scattered with Greek farms. The coastal strip and the open plains became Hellenized very soon. The new city-states were known as πόλεις Ἑλληνίδες, Hellenic cities (Diod. XVI. 73.2). Except for the few and sporadic moments of initial conflicts, we can hardly speak of any relationships between the indigenous populations and the Greek newcomers in this region of the Chalcidian colonies. Voluntarily or not, the Sicels simply disappeared from the stage, and πόλεις and χῶρα became Greek.

Archaeological material from the time immediately before the Greek landing is lacking in Catane, but in Leontini on the hill of Metapiccola substantial traces of a pre-Greek village have lately come to light.[1] The huts are like those on the Palatine in Rome, and the pottery contains both Apennine forms and typical late Iron Age types of Sicilian material (Fig. 10). In my opinion, they

Fig. 10. Indigenous pottery from Leontini

are the immediate and direct predecessors of the Greek installation. Of the latter there are traces in a wash layer below Colle di S. Mauro (Fig. 11), unfortunately without any direct connection with architectural remains. It is proto-Corinthian Geometric ceramic of the third quarter of the eighth century, fitting the historic foundation date of Leontini. These two groups of remains are neatly separated in style but are probably overlapping in time. In one case they are purely indigenous and in the other equally purely Greek. Apparently they are the remains of the period just before and just after the Greek takeover, and there are no connections between the two. Historically speaking, this means that the indigenous Sicels, after a brief coexistence with the Greeks, withdrew and disappeared rather tracelessly when the Greek settlers became permanently installed. From having been Sicel, Leontini became Greek, after a possible short period of symbiosis. A literary source (Polyaenus, *Strategemata* V. 5.1) indicates actually such an early coexistence (τοὺς συνοικοῦντας Σικελούς).

In order to study the development of the relations between Chalcidian Greeks and indigenous Sicels, we have to leave the fertile plain and move up toward the foothills of the Hyblaean and the Heraean mountains, whither the Sicels withdrew. The routes we have to follow are indicated by the small river valleys which all converge toward the plain and drain into the water system of Simeto, Dittaino, and Gornalunga.

Our first place to investigate is Licodia Eubea, situated in the Hyblaean mountains north of the watershed of the stream Dirillo which joins the draining system of the Gela Plain. Paolo Orsi excavated in 1898,[2] and later on in 1909,[3] a series of tombs, which are of interest to our inquiry, although tombs alone can never illustrate a cultural and historical development. For that, one needs a careful excavation of the settlement itself.

Orsi's publications are summary, but, as always, clear, conscientious, and learned. Unfortunately, they are illustrated in such a way that slide reproductions are out of the question. Some of the tombs had been plundered in modern times, but some were found intact. They were rock-cut chamber tombs used as family graves, following an indigenous, non-Greek usage. Only a few of them are single tombs in the Greek tradition.[4] The grave gifts accompanying the burials are of highly interesting and characteristic kinds. There are about equal numbers of purely Greek vases of late Corinthian and Attic manufacture of the latter half of the sixth century B.C. and of local Siculo-Geometric pottery. There is also a certain number of so-called Ionian cups which with all probability were manufactured in imitation of the genuine Greek ware, either in the πόλεις Ἑλληνίδες on the coast or actually *in loco* by Greek settlers.

But were any Greek settlers here in the sixth century B.C., or have we to deal only with Greek imports into an independent Sicel city? Orsi is convinced of the latter alternative, and he is lately followed by Vallet.[5] Their arguments are mainly two: 1) The type of tomb is basically non-Greek and native. 2) The indigenous Geometric pottery which makes up more than half of the grave gifts never occurs in Greek tombs at the coast or in well-established Greek secondary colonies such as Acrae and Camarina. "It is more than unlikely," says Orsi, "that the Greeks, who were so refined and advanced in the field of ceramics, would have accepted this inferior barbaric stuff."[6]

I respect Orsi's arguments, but I venture to be of another opinion. The evidence from Licodia Eubea itself is not sufficient to prove that the other alternative — that of the presence of Greek settlers — is preferable, but on the strength of the results gained in Morgantina, it is decidedly reinforced. We will have to return to this problem, and it may suffice for the moment to say that if we had Greek settlers in Licodia Eubea, they must have lived in close coexistence and in mutual respect with the Sicels. As a result, Sicel products were accepted as household and grave goods, and the Greeks partially modified their own traditional burial customs to comply with local Sicel habits.

The next site where we can trace Chalcidian influence or penetration into the interior of the island is Grammichele, situated in the foothills of the Heraean mountains east of the present town of Caltagirone. We are here also walking in the footsteps of the indefatigable Paolo Orsi who excavated on the site in 1897 and 1907.[7] There are tombs, as in Licodia, both of the Sicel and the Greek type in a joint cemetery, and their contents are much like those of Licodia: Siculo-Geometric, Corinthian, Attic, and local archaic Greek types. The indigenous pottery, however, is not quite as frequent as in Licodia.

The other important finds from Grammichele come from the ruined and plundered deposits of votive gifts from two small sanctuaries, the architecture of which

Fig. 11. Imported Greek pottery from Leontini

has entirely disappeared.[8] The architectural terracottas and the ex-votos span a period of time from the second quarter of the sixth century B.C. to the middle of the fifth century B.C.

A Gorgoneion antefix is in style quite reminiscent of some of our finds from Morgantina and belongs to the third quarter of the sixth century, while this splendid seated goddess (Fig. 12) belongs to the very end of the same century. Among the latest finds in the votive deposit is a female head with elegantly stylized hairdo, belonging to the middle of the fifth century.

Here, even Orsi feels that we have to deal with Greek settlers,[9] and it is hard to avoid such a conclusion. While the final proof can only come from the excavation of the town itself, the antefix testifies to the presence of a naïskos of Greek type, and the votive gifts indicate clearly and

Fig. 12. Terracotta figurine of seated goddess from Grammichele

indisputably Greek-Sicilian workmanship. The most remarkable imported piece is a Greek marble kouros (Fig. 13) of very high quality. It belongs to Gisela Richter's Ptoon 20 Group and should date to the years around 500 B.C.[10] Such a piece was a Greek ex-voto, and it could not have found its way into an indigenous settlement of Sicels, even if they were under great Greek cultural influence. It confirms, in my opinion, the Hellenic character of the lost city of Grammichele, which may have carried the name of Echetla[11] in ancient times.

The above information provides us with an example of Chalcidian penetration of the interior of Sicily, and it tells us something of the methods the Cataneans and/or Leontinians used in Hellenizing their part of central Sicily. It can be reconstructed in approximately this way.[12]

Sometime toward the end of the first quarter of the sixth century, when both Catane and Leontini had been established Greek centers for more than a century and a half, enterprising groups of men set off toward the interior and worked their way up the small river valleys in the Hyblaean and Heraean foothills. They belonged, most probably, to the latecomers of the coastal colonists, the ἔποικοι, artisans, merchants, and soldiers who longed for a more independent existence than the old oligarchic frame of the metropolis could offer them. They seem to have agreed easily with the local Sicels, and their joint settlement was probably characterized by peaceful coexistence. The common burial place and the free interchange of indigenous ceramic products with Greek imports and imitations speak decidedly for such a procedure.

It should be remembered that with the Greeks came, of course, the Greek language and Greek way of life, Greek art forms and political institutions. That lies in the nature of things when representatives of a sophisticated culture, convinced of their own superiority, come into contact and establish cooperation with the population of an underdeveloped area. Such an encounter is never quite free of conflicts, but the common and reciprocal advantages may soon have been realized by both parties, and a peaceful development under Hellenic leadership may have come into being.

This is how one would like to see the beginning of the Hellenization of central Sicily when a peaceful pattern was followed.

I want to repeat that Licodia Eubea and Grammichele cannot provide us with the airtight proof of such

a sequence of events, but I consider them both strong indicators in that direction. It should also be pointed out that our literary sources tell us nothing of this secondary colonization of the interior from coastal bases. However, although explicit factual information is lacking in the literature, I believe that the ancient texts give indirect but clear hints of this eminently important historical process.

In colonial contexts we are acquainted with certain terms which have already been discussed and to some extent are self-explanatory: μητρόπολις, the mother city in the Greek homeland; ἀποικία, a sovereign and independent colonial foundation in a foreign land, founded on all the customary religious and ritual ceremonies (τὰ νομιζόμενα); ἔποικοι, the latecomers from home who were accepted with or without various privileges in the recently founded colonies.

Besides these terms we meet often the word κληρουχία. A κληρουχία was a settlement not in foreign barbaric lands, but on soil conquered by one Greek πόλις from another, a fruit of one city-state's power expansion at the expense of another. The κληροῦχοι became freeholders not as pioneers but as conquerors. Such a term has obviously no application to our problem and can, for the time being, be left out of our discussion.

We have, however, reason to dwell on a fifth term which may help to clarify the problem. That is κτίσμα or κτίσις. The term sounds very noncommittal and means literally only the "foundation" or "building" of a city or a settlement. What it really means from the point of view of political status, dependency on a mother city, or freedom of political action has never been investigated, indeed hardly even observed. The small Greek city of Metauros, whose only claim to fame was that it became the birthplace of Stesichorus, is referred to in our texts as a κτίσμα Λοκρῶν, a foundation of Locri. It was thus a secondary colony from Locri Epizephyrii in Calabria, itself an Achaean colony from Greece. Metauros has no known founder, and its political privileges and affiliations are unknown, but they are in no way identical with those of an ἀποικία. The two terms are never used alternatively to describe one and the same colonial settlement, as far as I have been able to find out. It seems to apply to secondary colonies, founded without any pomp and circum-

Fig. 13. Greek marble torso from Grammichele

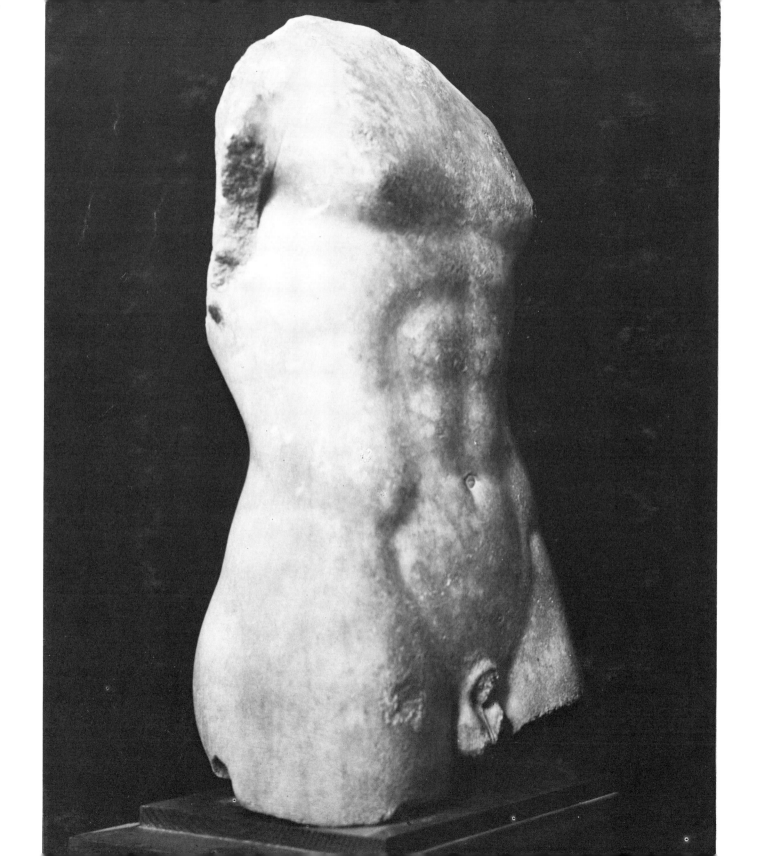

stance, without the official sanction of the mother city and without a specially appointed founder. It was a function of natural colonial expansion and of further penetration into more or less unknown barbaric land. The mother city did not give any official blessing of the enterprise, nor did it put its own prestige at stake. The driving force was the enterprising spirit of private citizens or their discontent with the political and economic conditions of their mother city, or both.

If this is the case, the κτίσματα played a very important rôle in the Hellenization of a colonial region. Small urban units, planted in strategic or otherwise valuable sites by private citizens, must have contributed immeasurably to the spread of the Greek way of life in barbaric lands. Their small size and their remoteness must have accelerated the process of amalgamation between the Greeks and the indigenous populations. They may have acted as a potent ferment for the fusion of the two ethnic groups through intermarriage and cultural interchange.

Licodia Eubea and Grammichele may have been two such Chalcidian κτίσματα, but in these cases the archaeological proofs are insufficient. I believe that a third place — Morgantina — still further inland and still more remote

from the beaten track may provide us with fuller and safer information. It is the only central Sicilian site that has been systematically excavated and studied under a long-range program and that has yielded sanctuaries and a settlement, as well as tombs. This trinity provides us with a possibility of gaining an overall view of its historical development and character which we now have to consider briefly.

Morgantina lies practically in the geographical center of the island, at the watershed between the rivers Gela and Gornalunga. The only natural way of access to the mountainous place follows the river valley from the east. The hill town faces the east and overlooks the Catania Plain with the towering Mount Etna in the far background.

A contour level map shows how well defended the place is by nature and demonstrates also that the area of the town consists of an acropolis, still called by the local farmers "la Cittadella," as well as a long, narrow built-up area to the west of it, now called *Serra Orlando* (Fig. 14).

The acropolis was the oldest nucleus of the town, and it is there we can gather our information on its early history. It is a very steep hill with a top plateau and a lower spur on the northeast side. The lower spur has, so far, given us the oldest Greek remains.[13]

Fig. 14. Contour level map of Morgantina

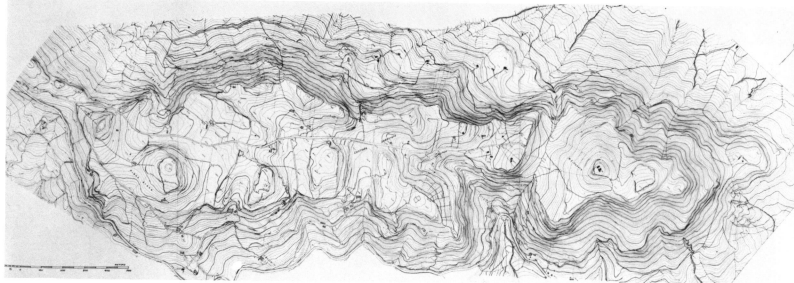

Fig. 15. Sicel hut found under the Greek terracotta dump on the lower acropolis of Morgantina

Fig. 16. Greek archaic wall on the lower acropolis of Morgantina

In one of our trenches we came upon a massive deposit of architectural terracottas and roof tiles. The way in which these masses of debris were found tells us that we are confronted with a dump of discarded material from a destroyed or dismantled little temple, which must have stood somewhere in the neighborhood. After lifting this deposit we came upon the remains of a sizable Sicel hut or small house where the pottery found was exclusively Siculo-Geometric material (Fig. 15).

This is not an ideal stratigraphic situation, as can well be imagined. One cannot safely judge the lapse of time between the collapse and abandonment of the Sicel hut and the dumping of the Greek debris. As a matter of fact, the dumping — as we learned from other observations — took place in the last part of the sixth century B.C., and at that time the hut must have long since been abandoned.

The antecedents of the story could be read in a neighboring trench. This fine ashlar wall,[14] which served as a retaining wall of the temple terrace, is unmistakably of Greek workmanship with pry-holes and anathyrosis (Fig. 16). It consists of two sections: the original, carefully built part and a continuation built of reused material, including the two hawksbeak blocks from over the doorway of a small temple (Fig. 17). The prolongation of the wall must, therefore, have been built in connection with the dismantling of the original temple. At the same time, its roof elements were dumped over the site of the neighboring Sicel hut. The secondary construction must have been caused by an emergency when sacred building material was used for defense purposes and when the holy place was hastily transformed into a bastion.

The stage preceding the building of the fine sacred terrace wall can well be studied in this figure. The terrace wall was laid over a set of house foundations after the houses had been destroyed. These houses were, again, Siculo-Geometric and contained only one imported Greek vase, a small Middle Corinthian eye aryballos, datable to approximately 575–550 B.C.

A section through the area tells the story with great

Fig. 17. Reused blocks in archaic wall on the lower acropolis of Morgantina

Fig. 18. Section through a trench at Morgantina

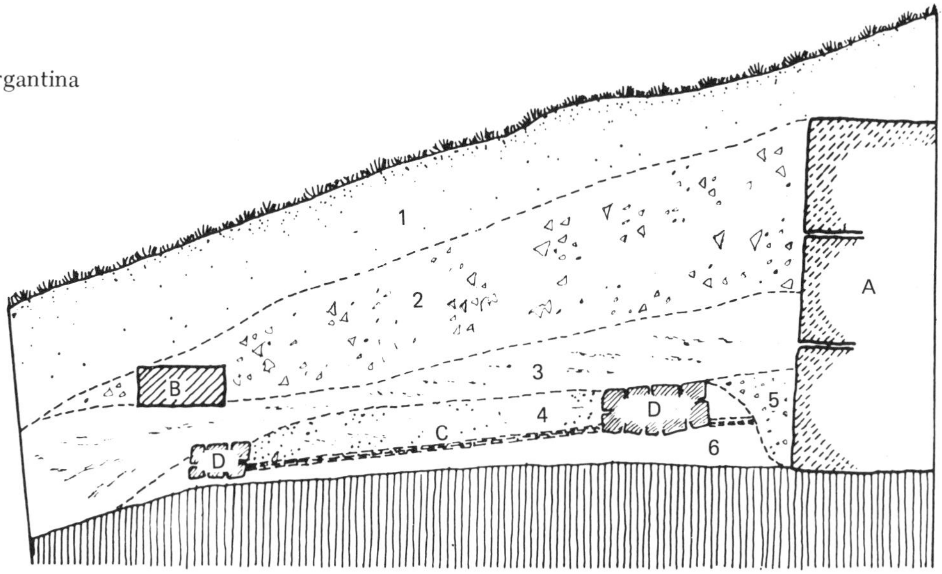

Fig. 19. Archaic houses on upper
acropolis of Morgantina

clarity (Fig. 18). The foundation trench of the terrace wall (5) cuts right through the preceding structure (4 and C-D), the floor deposit of which showed signs of conflagration and contained the usual Siculo-Geometric material. The terrace wall could be dated, thanks to the presence of Attic black figure ware (the bottom of a little master's cup), to 560–550 B.C.

We have thus come to the joint between two cultural horizons, the indigenous and the Greek, and have evidence for fixing it in time at the end of the second quarter of the sixth century B.C.

At the same time, the main upper plateau of the acropolis also changed its appearance. Instead of scattered indigenous huts, we find a complex of regularly built houses with narrow streets and small squares (Fig. 19).

The late Middle Corinthian pyxis (Fig. 20), found under the street level, may serve as a synchronizer.

Architectural terracottas which once decorated the many small shrines on the acropolis proper abound:

Gorgo antefix	c. 550 B.C. (Fig. 21)
Gorgo antefix	c. 525 B.C. (Fig. 22)
Gorgo antefix	c. 500 B.C. (Fig. 23)
Maenad antefix	c. 550 B.C. (Fig. 24)

We deal here with artifacts of clearly Greek style and iconography, although admittedly crude in execution. They are all molded, and some of them were retouched by a sculptor's tool before firing. Were the molds brought from the coast or were they, as was the final product,

Fig. 20. Corinthian pyxis from upper acropolis of Morgantina

Fig. 21. Gorgoneion antefix
from Morgantina, c. 550 B.C.

Fig. 22. Gorgoneion antefix from Morgantina, c. 525 B.C.

Fig. 23. Gorgoneion antefix from Morgantina, c. 500 B.C.

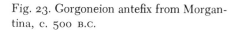

Fig. 24. Maenad antefix from Morgantina, c. 550 B.C.

Fig. 25. Ridge pole tiles from lower acropolis of Morgantina

Fig. 26. Sima with drain spouts from lower acropolis
of Morgantina

modeled locally? There are no specimens known to me which repeat these forms, so I believe that we have reason to assume that the molds were local products. The newcomers did not bring with them koroplasts of the first order, but talented artisans who developed their own peripheral but vigorous Greek styles.

From the dump above the Sicel hut we were able to reconstruct the elements of the roof (Fig. 25). Finally, there also came the better part of a sima with water spouts, which proves better than anything else (Fig. 26) that the small temples of Morgantina were of the same type as their purely Greek counterparts from the coastal cities.

There can no longer be any reasonable doubt that the sixth-century settlers of Morgantina were Greeks and originated from the Chalcidian colonies on the east coast.[15]

It should, however, be pointed out that the ceramic material found in this archaic πόλις is by no means exclusively Greek. Most of the simple jars and vases, intended for everyday household use, were of local Sicel production. The Siculo-Geometric pottery can be followed through at least two centuries as a parallel phenomenon to the Greek vases.

This speaks strongly for the assumption that Greeks and Sicels lived in peace with one another and cooperated for the common weal.

We can see evidence for this in the archaic necropolis located on the northeastern slopes of the acropolis.[16] The tombs were rock-cut chamber tombs of the type which Orsi found at Licodia Eubea. They were family tombs used by subsequent generations and not single shafts or sarcophagus tombs according to the common Greek system.

Our Tomb 4,[17] which contained the remains of at least seven skeletons and over two hundred grave gifts, extends in time from about 520 to 480 B.C. This wealthy burial can hardly have belonged to a native, particularly as over half of the burial gifts were of Greek manufacture. They included an Attic vase, an Attic lekythos, and Ionian cups, found side by side with Siculo-Geometric ware: a Siculo-Geometric amphora, a Siculo-Geometric pitcher, and local imitations of Greek ware.

It should also be mentioned that in the same necropolis one tomb showed a clearly Greek burial rite.[18] It was a cremation tomb with the ash urn sunk in a pit in the rock and a covered shaft close to it with the burial gifts. The ashes of the dead Greek were, however, gathered in a Siculo-Geometric amphora.

We may now be ready for some conclusions.

The Chalcidian colonies on the east coast played a great and important rôle in the early Hellenization of the interior. Thucydides was right when telling us that, even in his own days at the end of the fifth century, the Sicels inhabited the central and northern parts of the island, but he did not tell us that as early as in the first half of the sixth century there were also Greeks occupying these territories.

We needed archaeological evidence to reach that conclusion. There is still more exploration needed in this field before the picture is fully developed, but I believe that we already can discern an Ionian-Chalcidian pattern followed in their Hellenization of the interior. Their small κτίσματα were sent out, not as official claimers of land and political sovereignity, but as free enterprises of private citizens in quest for a better and freer form of life. They were not in principle bellicose conquerors, but basically peaceful penetrators. Morgantina built no defense walls until the last quarter of the sixth century B.C., when the political climate in this region had sharpened considerably. They brought with them their Greek heritage unadulterated, and we can trace it in their city planning, their sanctuaries, and their religious customs. They brought with them their language and their philosophy of life and became, on the strength of their cultural superiority, the unquestioned leaders of the newly founded cities. They grew wealthy from the rich soil, from the thick forests, and from trade, and they gave their region a new life and a new prosperity.

The indigenous Sicels probably played a secondary rôle in the society, but they were not eradicated or suppressed. The cooperation between the two ethnic elements brought about a quick and durable Hellenization of the Sicels and did not leave the Greek element entirely unaffected, to judge from the tomb forms in Licodia Eubea and Morgantina. These friendly relations between Chalcidian colonists and indigenous populations had, as we shall see later on, its healthy repercussions far down into the politically troublesome fifth century B.C.

4 The Dorians and Their Secondary Colonies in Sicily

We were able to trace in Chapter 3 what I would call the Chalcidian system of cultural penetration of central Sicily, and we found that it followed a relatively peaceful and unobtrusive pattern, as far as it has become archaeologically tested. Small κτίσματα or foundations of Greek centers were planted on well-chosen sites like Licodia Eubea, Grammichele, and Morgantina, and from them radiated the benefits of Greek civilization. Conflicts with the Sicels were avoided, and a friendly coexistence of the two ethnic groups resulted in a rapid Hellenization of the Sicels and an equally rapid increase of the general prosperity of the cities and their territories under Greek leadership.

The Chalcidian penetration was an unofficial, spontaneous move in which we can trace no direct political or territorial designs of government or state character, but rather a quest for land and better living conditions by groups of enterprising private citizens.[1] And yet, of the new centers we know that at least Morgantina grew big and important enough to mark its independence and sovereignty by striking silver coins as early as the first half of the fifth century B.C. The results of the Chalcidian penetration were very positive and seemingly stable, but the methods applied for reaching them were mild and elastic.

The Dorians in Syracuse, Gela, and Agrigentum do not seem to have followed the same system as the Chalcidians of Catane and Leontini. It is to these Dorians that we now turn our attention.

Thucydides (VI. 3.2) tells us that the Corinthians under Archias had to fight with the native Sicels for the possession of the island Ortygia. To the survivors of the indigenous population in Syracuse itself and to the original inhabitants of the quickly growing Greek territory was reserved a sad function in the colony's economic and social structure. They became a low caste group, called the Killyrioi, and had to live as the new master's serfs, tilling the fields of the γαμόροι, the Greek aristocratic landowners.

Under these circumstances it is no wonder that the Syracusans' penetration into the hinterland had to overcome a stubborn resistance put up by the local Sicels. Megara Hyblaea and the Chalcidian colonies blocked the Syracusan expansion toward the big Catania Plain to the north and northwest because they preceded them, and it is only natural that the Syracusan efforts were concentrated in the opposite direction of south and southwest. Due west, up the Anapos River valley, they encountered the Sicel stronghold of Pantalica which must have discouraged them from frontal attack for some time at least.

The map (Fig. 27) illustrates better than words the topographical situation and the roads of access to the interior which the Syracusans followed. It was made by Antonio di Vita who has dedicated a thorough study to our problem.[2] The southern outpost of Helorus was settled before the year 600 B.C. It carries in Aelian (*De Animalibus*, XII. 30) the denomination of φρούριον Συρακοσίων, a fortress of the Syracusans, and it certainly does not carry its name in vain.

It was a military and strategic installation on a steep hill at the mouth of the Helorus River (present-day Tellaro).[3] Helorus does not only secure the road southward, but it also cuts off in a very efficient way the great Sicel center of Finocchito higher up in the valley. φρούριον is thus a new term used in connection with Sicilian colonial affairs, and the term is self-explanatory. It was a military fortress and should thus be considered as something different from a κτίσμα, which merely meant a settlement. This does not mean that a κτίσμα could not be fortified or serve military purposes as well, but it should be remembered that Morgantina was, from the beginning, an open city while Helorus was just a fortress.

In 663 B.C., seventy years after the foundation of Syracuse, and probably even before Helorus was occupied, the Syracusans sent out their first secondary colony of which our sources speak. It is Acrae, the present-day Palazzuolo-Acreide. This place also served from the beginning military and strategic purposes. It was well fortified from the start[4] and was so placed as to neutralize and isolate the Sicel town of Pantalica to the north. In spite of its very considerable size and its pretentious urban lay-out, it did not strike coins of its own until Roman provincial times. This is in contrast to the more modest κτίσμα of Morgantina and shows that it was under tight Syracusan control. The installation of Acrae opened the way for explorations still further west, and it served as a springboard for what seems to have been a master plan of further Syracusan conquests.

Acrae was a completely Greek city. Settlement and tombs have not brought to light any Sicel pottery or other artifacts, and the burial customs were purely Greek. We have no signs of Greco-Siculan coexistence. This could

hardly be expected under the circumstances.

The march to the west went on. Twenty years after Acrae, i.e., ninety years after the foundation of the mother city, the Syracusans were ready for their next leap forward. Then, says Thucydides (VI. 5.2), Casmenae was founded in 643 B.C.

There has been much discussion over the placement of Casmenae, but Di Vita[5] has proved to my satisfaction that it should be identified with the famous Monte Casale. Orsi excavated sporadically on the site, but, for once, he never found time to publish his results. Casmenae was, and is still, a singularly inhospitable settlement, but quite appropriate from a military point of view. Situated inaccessibly on a plateau 830 meters above sea level, its winter climate is very hard and its summers scorching hot. It was made impregnable by a solid fortification wall, and the town plan was rigidly regular with a rectangular street grid. In one part of the town, there was a temple of distinctly archaic type. In the temenos was found a votive deposit consisting of not fewer than six hundred iron spearheads, swords, and other weapons.[6] They were the ex-votos of the Greek garrison and underscore the preponderantly military character of this site.

From a strategic point of view, it caught the remaining Sicel stronghold of Hybla Heraea (present-day Ragusa) in the rear and opened the way to the fertile triangle along the coast between the rivers Ippari and Dirillo. This was as far west as Syracuse could push without coming into direct conflict with the Geloans whose territorial border followed the Dirillo River.

Casmenae and Acrae played their rôle in internal Syracusan politics and were seemingly always very dependent on the mother city. They were the military outposts of the growing Syracusan territory in a hostile Sicel hinterland. In the mountains between them, we may count on smaller military installations of the φρούριον type, like Helorus. Acrillae was one of them, and Di Vita[7] has correctly located it at the present-day Chiaramonte.

Of a very different type was the third subcolony founded by Syracuse, Camarina.[8] Its foundation took place in 598 B.C., forty-five years after Casmenae (Thucy. VI. 5.3), at a time, in other words, when the hinterland was militarily controlled by Syracuse and the logistics were safe. It was placed along the south coast in the west corner of the fertile triangle limited by the rivers Ippari and Dirillo. Camarina had founders of her own, Daskon

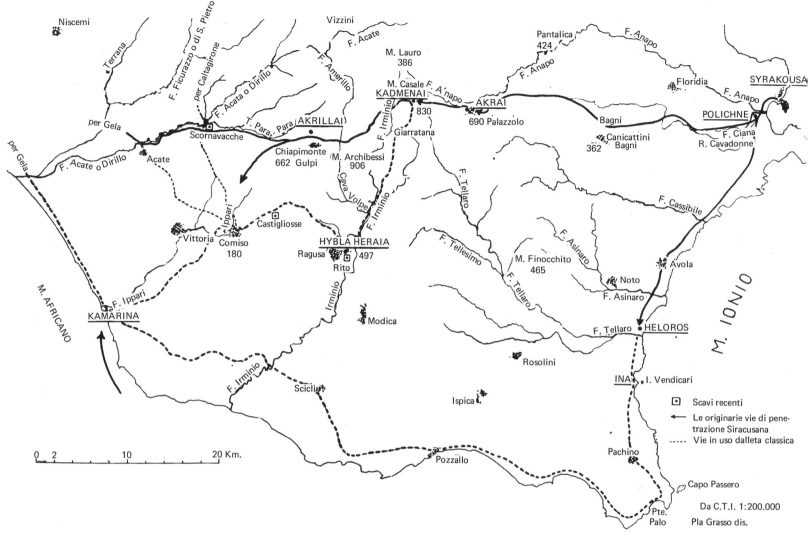

Fig. 27. Map showing the expansion of Syracusan territory in archaic times (after Di Vita)

and Menekolos, who might conceivably have been called in directly from the ultimate mother city, Corinth, in Greece. In any case, Camarina's position was much freer in relation to Syracuse than those of Acrae and Casmenae. It had also great material possibilities, situated as it was on the coast with an acceptable harbor and in the midst of a rich agricultural area.

Camarina was surrounded by Sicel mountain tribes and settlements who had all suffered considerably from the oppressive Syracusan policy. The colonists evidently understood that their very existence depended on better relationships with their immediate neighbors and, above all, with the inhabitants of the Sicel stronghold of Hybla Heraea (Ragusa). The site was excavated by Orsi in 1891 and 1898[9] and more recently by Di Vita.[10] The tombs contained grave gifts of the mixed Greek and Siculo-Geometric type we know from Licodia Eubea and Morgantina. Di Vita's[11] excavation of the necropolis of Rito is situated in the foothills just below Hybla Heraea itself and testifies to the beginning of peaceful relations some time soon after the foundation of Camarina.[12]

That these relations developed rapidly and brought Camarina to hostile action against Syracuse finds flagrant expression in the open revolt of Camarina against its mother city. It broke out in 553 B.C. On that occasion, the Sicels fought on the side of the Camarinaeans. They were defeated at the River Hyrminos, close to Hybla Heraea.[13] That defeat spelled the first destruction of Camarina and probably the last attempt of the Sicels of this region to achieve a better treatment from the Syracusans. After the battle of Hyrminos Syracuse was unrivaled mistress of the entire southeast corner of the island and bordered directly on the Geloan territory.

During this period Gela, founded by Rhodians and Cretans in 688 B.C., had rapidly grown in power and prosperity. Of all the Greek coastal cities in Sicily, none is more thoroughly explored than Gela, the original hometown of the mighty dynasty of the Deinomenids. Orsi worked there in early days, and during the last two decades the three archaeologists Griffo, Adamesteanu, and Orlandini under Griffo have formed an ideal team of explorers, not only of Gela itself, but also of its vast hinterland. They have provided us with much precious material apt to shed light on our problem.

So many are the places surveyed or excavated that space does not allow us to consider them all in detail.

Some of the more important sites should, however, be briefly analyzed here.

The first major site to discuss is Butera,[14] situated on the very border of the Geloan Plain, northwest of the city itself. Here Adamesteanu excavated a stratified necropolis, two upper layers of which are of fourth and third century dates. The other two go back to the time of the foundation of Gela in the seventh century B.C. The graves contain only indigenous Sicel pottery. "Dans toutes les tombes fouillées on n'a trouvé aucun vase grec," says the excavator.[15] The gap in the sequence of the tombs, from the end of the seventh to the end of the fourth centuries, seems to me to indicate a hiatus in the history of the settlement.

The indigenous pottery is all wheelmade and betrays in its forms and technique a certain Greek influence as does all native pottery of this period, but it is hard to believe that the manufacturers were any but indigenous Sicels. The abrupt end of this production indicates, in my opinion, that the ethnic group responsible for it was either chased away or enslaved or eradicated by the Geloans. It must have happened at an early stage in the colony's history. The annihilation of the Butera settlement which dominated the plain at close quarters must have seemed a dire necessity to the new settlers who could not have tilled their fields in peace under the eyes of hostile Sicels well entrenched on the Butera hill. It does not seem to have been resettled until the fourth century B.C. when the political situation was profoundly changed.

The anonymous site of Monte Bubbonia may have, perhaps, a better claim on the name of Maktorion, but even in this case, the denomination must remain quite hypothetical. It is a well fortified place,[16] situated in a strategic position guarding the mountain pass which leads further inland toward what I would call the Chalcidian region of penetration north and west of Caltagirone. It has a sister installation of the same type further east at Monte San Mauro.[17] These two fortresses could effectively dominate and control the inland route, serving in addition as spearheads for further penetration inland.

One is reminded of the φρούρια τῶν Ἑλλήνων, the fortresses of the Greeks, that so often meet us in Diodorus's narration of events in this area of the island (Diod. XI. 91, XIX. 110). These Greek fortified sites are sometimes mentioned in contrast to the φρούρια τῶν Σικελῶν, the fortresses of the Sicels. The nomenclature seems to indi-

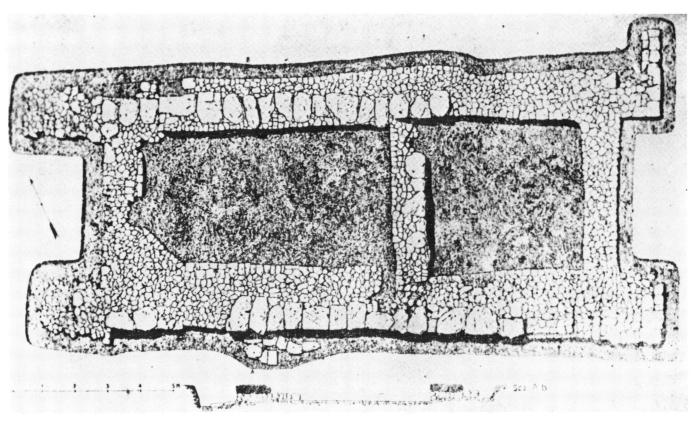

Fig. 28. Foundations of naïskos at Monte San Mauro

cate that a great deal of fighting went on in these parts of Sicily, and that the Geloan penetration of the interior was far from peaceful.

Monte Bubbonia and Monte San Mauro, the latter probably to be identified as the city of Omphake, mentioned by Stephanus Byzantinus quoting Timaeus and by Pausanias (VIII. 46.2), are both purely Greek installations of considerable size. Both show traces of preceding indigenous settlements violently destroyed by the conquering Greeks. Neither is in any way fully excavated. Orsi worked there in 1905–1911,[18] and Adamesteanu in 1955.[19] They have, however, yielded a sufficient number of finds and monuments to allow for safe conclusions. Some time in the middle of the sixth century B.C. the Greeks settled on these hills, fortified them in a solid way, and built their small temples and regular houses within the perimeter of the protecting walls.

After the Greek takeover there are no traces of the Sicel indigenous population, as we find it in Grammichele, Licodia Eubea, and Morgantina. The forms of the sacred architecture and of its decoration are Geloan in character. A comparison between the naïskos at Monte San Mauro (Fig. 28) and the earliest Athenaion in Gela seems, to me, quite conclusive albeit the two monuments have only survived in their bare foundations.

The terracotta revetment of the small temple in Monte Bubbonia included a Gorgo antefix of Geloan type.

A sima with waterspouts (Fig. 29),[20] here reconstructed in a design by Orsi's masterly draftsman, Rosario Carta, can be compared in detail with the entablature from the temple on the acropolis of Gela (Fig. 30)[21]

The houses at Monte Bubbonia were modest but of the regular Greek or megalo-Hellenic type with rectangular rooms adjacent to a fenced-in courtyard, forming the

Fig. 29. Sima with drain spouts from Monte San Mauro

Fig. 30. Sima from the Athena temple in Gela

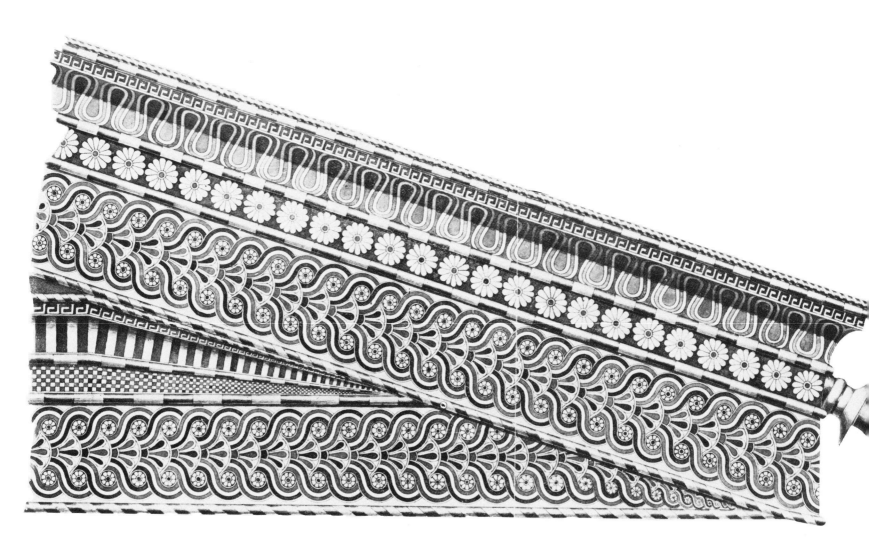

plan of a regular Greek small city, a πόλις or πολίχνιον as Diodorus calls the minor centers of the interior. They are radically different from the irregular agglomerations of huts that we meet in Sicily before the Greek colonization.

In addition, the tombs are of the normal Greek type: a single shaft covered by big roof tiles. The grave gifts consist of Corinthian and Attic vases or imitations of them. That Monte Bubbonia also had wealthy and important citizens is shown by a magnificent Corinthian bronze crater found in a clandestinely excavated tomb.

These two Geloan strongholds in the rather distant hinterland were backed by a whole series of similar fortified settlements closer to the coast. We know of their existence thanks to Adamesteanu's thorough survey and sporadic excavation: Monte Desusino, Lavanca Nero, Milingiana, and Monte Saraceno.[22]

They seem to indicate a systematic and formidable build-up, not only for a gradual colonization of the interior, but also for a regular conquest of it. The system of fortresses and well-defended settlements signifies that there were hostilities and resistance to be overcome, in the same way as was so clearly the case with Syracuse's domination of the southeast corner of Sicily.

When the sixth century came to an end, the Geloans were masters of a large and well-defended territory, from which we have very few material traces of the aboriginal population. The Sicels' existence must have been a very humble one. The picture again reminds us of the situation in the Syracusan hinterland, where their lot was that of serfdom and poverty. Under such conditions the cultural traditions and the artistic productivity of a people tend to die out and disappear. Such seems to have been the case in these two Dorian districts of Sicily.

The growth of Geloan power during the sixth century was steady and uninterrupted. In 580 B.C. Gela was ready to send out a regular colony of her own — Acragas-Agrigentum, one hundred and eight years after the landing of the Rhodians and Cretans. This was a decisive drive westwards and brought the Rhodio-Cretan power complex to the borders of Selinuntine territory at the River Halykos. Agrigentum itself grew into a legendarily wealthy city and came around the year 570 B.C. under the powerful rule of Phalaris, the tyrant of infamous renown.

From Agrigentum, the relentless drive toward the interior followed the valleys of the rivers Salso (ancient Himera) and Platani (Halykos). The pattern seems to have been basically the one set by the Geloans of the mother city. Thanks to the work of De Miro, Orlandini, and Adamesteanu,[23] we can follow their march, which is spotted with φρούρια of the now well-known Geloan type, fortified settlements that form two converging strings along the valleys and meet up in the central mountains at the watershed. They hold firmly in their grip the Sican territory squeezed in between them, although Sican resistance must have been felt on different occasions.

Among the countless anecdotes tied to Phalaris and his tyranny, there is one that may concern us here. Polyaenus (V. 1.4) tells the story of his conquest of a prosperous and large Sican town called Vessa, ruled by a certain Teuton. Asking for the hand of Teuton's daughter, Phalaris treacherously sent his soldiers dressed as bridesmaids and carrying gifts to the Sican chieftain. In this dishonorable way he became the master of Vessa, and Teuton met his death at the wedding feast of his own daughter.

The two names of Teuton and Vessa are not mentioned anywhere else in ancient literature, and Polyaenus must have got them from a source now lost.[24] They bring us for once a glimpse of Sican history. This and similar anecdotes may in themselves not be true, but their existence tells us something valuable about the early relationships between the Acragantines and the Sicans.

To return to Gela and the Sicels toward the end of the sixth century, the position of the former was as strong as that of the latter was weak. Gela's system of military bases was well built up and must have initiated further conquest.

This is the time when the first tyrant of Gela appears on the stage of history. He was Kleandros, son of Pantares. He belonged to the family of the Deinomenids which can be traced back to the earliest years of the colony. Tradition tells us that he ruled for seven years and was followed by his brother, Hippocrates. This happened approximately in 498 B.C.

With Hippocrates the dynamic forces of the Deinomenid dynasty got into motion. In 494 he entered for the first time victorious on the pan-Sicilian stage. This was the year when the Persians quelled the Ionian revolt and Miletus fell to Darius the Great. This event caused a great exodus of Ionian Greeks from the threatened East to the safer and happier West. Among them were the survivors of Miletus and a group of Samians. They sailed for Sicily on the invitation of the citizens of Zancle (Messina) who welcomed them as cosettlers of a planned subcolony called Caleacte. They betrayed their prospective hosts and occupied Zancle itself during the temporary absence of the Zancleans, who were besieging a Sicel town in the interior under the leadership of their "king," Scythes. The Zancleans called their ally, Hippocrates, for help, but on his arrival he sided with the invaders and left the Samians in possession of the town (Herod. VI. 23-25).

We hear of this crossing of the island by Hippocrates and his armed forces from Gela to Messina-Zancle in Herodotus as well (VII. 154). Here Herodotus gives us a better idea of the vast scope of Hippocrates' enterprise. This campaign carried him to victory over the following places, named by Herodotus in this order: Kallipolis, Naxos, Zancle-Messina, Leontini, and to the walls of Syracuse. Our author adds, "no city escaped submission, but Syracuse." The Syracusans were also beaten but were saved by the mediation of Corinth and Corcyra — at which time Camarina was given to Hippocrates.

This was by far the most spectacular demonstration of military strength ever displayed in the history of Greek Sicily. Looking at the map (Fig. 31), we cannot help noticing the seemingly erratic route Hippocrates followed: Kallipolis on the slopes of Etna (near Randazzo)

Fig. 31. Ancient route from Gela to the north

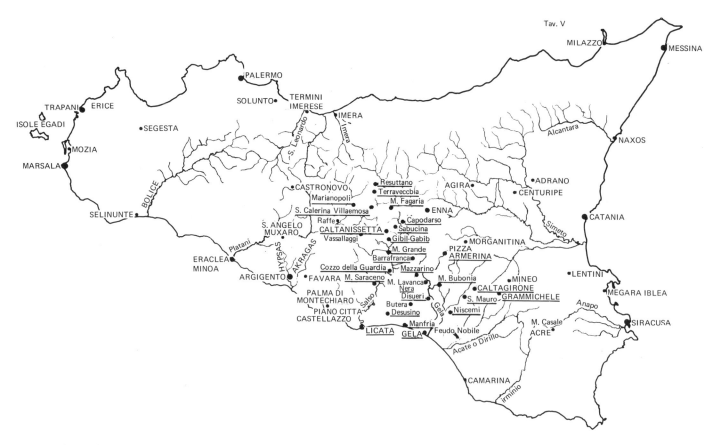

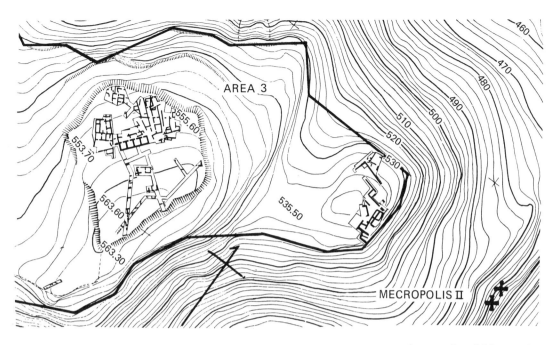

Fig. 32. Map of acropolis of Morgantina

was a Naxian κτίσμα; then Naxos (present-day Taormina), which means that he passed around Mount Etna; then up to Messina and south again to Leontini and Syracuse. The surprising mobility of his forces can be explained only by the presence of a network of roads that crossed over the island in every direction. Such a road system must have developed in the wake of the Greek penetration of the interior. It is obvious that if these roads could be traced in modern topography, we would be able to follow Hippocrates and his victorious troops more or less step by step.

Thanks to aerial photography undertaken on the initiative of, and interpreted by Adamesteanu, such a task is now feasible. Here are some of the results of this modern form of topographical research.[25] From their strong bases at Monte Bubbonia and Monte San Mauro the Geloans followed the route through the pass near Caltagirone. At the crossroads north of the pass, one route goes eastward to Leontini; the other continues north, in which direction Hippocrates marched, according to the information Herodotus gives us.

The first city of any importance on this northern route is Morgantina. There can be little doubt that

Hippocrates took it by force: "No city escaped submission, but Syracuse," says Herodotus (VII. 154).

Can the archaeological results gained in our excavations confirm and substantiate such an event? This seems to be the case.

It may be remembered that Morgantina was originally a Chalcidian κτίσμα of a seemingly peaceful character. No city wall protected the early settlement on the acropolis. The formation of the ground, the steep slopes, and the good relations with the Sicels were considered sufficient to secure its future. But when Hippocrates' army appeared in the valley to the south of the town, quick defense measures were asked for. On this occasion a wall already existed around the top plateau of the acropolis, including the lower acropolis (Fig. 32). On the latter, the old temple was incorporated into the defense system. The naïskos was hastily dismantled and the holy place turned into a bastion. As one can see on this section which was discussed earlier, the level was raised and some blocks from the old terrace wall were used for an outer rampart.

To place these hasty and panic-motivated actions in time is not entirely easy on the evidence from the lower

Fig. 33. Fallen roof tiles of naïskos in a trench at Morgantina

acropolis alone. It should be pointed out that the building of the acropolis wall may have taken place even somewhat earlier than the turn of the century. The Morgantinians may have had some presentiment of the aggressive Geloan policy and of the coming storm as early as the last quarter of the sixth century. The construction of the defense wall may well have been carried through as an orderly precaution, and not as an emergency action. This can, however, not have been the case with the desecration of the temple.

Another excavated area[26] west of the acropolis offers the possibility of checking these chronological assumptions.

In approximately 525 B.C. the Greek town had begun to spread from the acropolis to the neighboring ridge of Serra Orlando. Here one of our trenches proved very informative. A section through it tells an interesting story. This information is supplemented by a study of the plan. We deal here with a small archaic temple; although the

plan is not complete, we can see that it was of a very long and narrow type. No peristyle or columns were used. The eaves of the gabled roof were very wide, as can be gathered from the distance between the foundations and the gutter running parallel to the building. Our possibilities of dating it with some precision were increased by the way it underwent its sudden destruction. The superstructure of timber and mudbrick had gone up in flames and the entire roof had fallen in and remained *in situ* covering the floor (Fig. 33). The archaic wall was extant only in its foundations (Fig. 34). Outside the foundations were found a number of Gorgo antefixes of a relatively late sixth-century type, testifying to a construction date of approximately 525 B.C.

A quarter of a century after it had been built, the temple underwent its final and violent destruction, never to be built again. The destruction must be laid to Hippocrates and his Geloan forces.

The emergency fortifications on the acropolis seem

Fig. 34. Foundations of archaic naïskos
in a trench at Morgantina

to have been of no avail. What happened after the burning and plundering of the suburban temple can only be guessed. The outlying lower acropolis and the main acropolis area show no signs of wholesale destruction. Life seems to have continued on the Cittadella more or less as it had gone before. I am inclined to conclude that the Morgantinians opened their gates to the conqueror and that the city became a part of the Deinomenid power structure. If that were the case, we have reached a decisive turn in the history of our town and of the Chalcidian κτίσματα of the interior.

From then onward, Morgantina became a Doric city. The name itself with the final alpha, instead of eta, shows that the inhabitants spoke a Doric dialect. This is confirmed by all the inscriptions found on our site. Such a change was probably brought about by bringing in Geloan κληροῦχοι as landowners and masters of the town.

The first conquering Deinomenid made, indeed, a great impact on the Hellenism of central Sicily, bringing to an abrupt end the Chalcidian-Ionian chapter of peaceful penetration and Greco-Sicel coexistence.

But Hippocrates marched further, and his route can be traced beyond Morgantina. Here in this aerial photo (Fig. 35), it can be seen heading due north toward Agira and beyond to Kallipolis and Naxos, Zancle, Catane, and Leontini. The latter were the Chalcidian mother cities of Morgantina and shared the fate of their outlying κτίσματα in the central mountains.

In these years the old Chalcidian colonies lost much of their political power and their territories to the conquering Deinomenids. The Geloans of Cretan origin expanded victorious over the better part of the island. Their quick rise from relative obscurity to powerful masters of Sicily in the latter half of the sixth century needed some mythical historical motivation. This, I would suggest, could be the time when they remembered the early greatness of their mother island under King Minos in the heroic age. In these years of ruthless expansion, they felt a need of legendary motivation for their conquests, and so the myth of Cocalos and Minos was created. The city name of Minoa may have been the starting point of the aetiological myth. In the name of the conquest of the island by Minos, and as a revenge for his ignominious death at the hands of the Sicans, their military conquests and their oppressive policy became historically founded and motivated. They were only regaining what were their ancestral rights and property, and revenging injuries their forebears had undergone in the past.

In that sense, mythical legend and military action met and fused into a new political reality.

Fig. 35. Ancient route from Morgantina to Agyrium. Air photography

5 Greeks, Carthaginians, and Sicels in the Fifth and Fourth Centuries B.C.

The beginning of the fifth century was a critical period in the history of Hellenism both in the East and the West. In those years, the Ionian revolt was quelled by the Persian Great King, and the Greek cities on the west coast of Asia Minor passed under Persian rule. The Persians prepared themselves very carefully to deal a final blow also to the Greek motherland, and thus the Persian Wars began. The unforeseen and almost incredible results were the battles of Marathon and Salamis, which saved Greece from becoming a Persian satrapy and initiated the greatest century in the history of Greek civilization.

Not only the Greek East and the motherland itself were in grave danger in those years. Sicily and the West also had to fight for their existence.

Herodotus (VII. 157–164) gives us a lively and seemingly reliable account of the events before the outbreak of the second Persian War. Spartan and Athenian envoys reached Syracuse and pleaded with Gelon for help in the approaching danger. They did so in the name of pan-Hellenism and of the solidarity which ought to exist between mother country and colonies. Gelon's answer was haughty but not negative. It contained a condition unacceptable to both Spartans and Athenians — that they should make him commander-in-chief of the united forces. In reading Gelon's answer carefully, one gains the impression that the Syracusans had been left without help on an earlier occasion when they had invited the Spartans to join them in a war against the Carthaginians (VII. 158).[1] This event, which is difficult to place in time with any precision, would then have been the earliest recorded open conflict between Greeks and Carthaginians in Sicily.

The next was soon to come. Herodotus and Diodorus (XI. 21) are our sources. Internal strife in the city of Himera on the north coast had caused the expelled tyrant, Terillus, to call for Carthaginian help to obtain his restoration to power. His son-in-law, Anaxilas of Rhegium, made common cause with him, and the great war between Gelon and Carthage broke out. Technically speaking, it was not a Carthaginian aggression, because they were asked to intervene by dissenting Greeks, but from the Syracusan point of view, their task was doubtless to defend the Greek island against a barbarian invasion.

This was exactly what Gelon and his Agrigentine ally, Theron, did with great brilliance. The famous battle of Himera in 480 B.C. ended in a catastrophic annihilation of the Carthaginian forces under Hamilcar. To mark the equivalent importance of the Greek victories at Salamis and Himera, legend would have it that they were fought on the same day (Herod. VII. 166).

At Himera Syracuse had secured her hegemony over Sicily in a very convincing way and acquired for herself a solid position of power in the whole Hellenic world. The Deinomenid dynasty of Syracuse dominated the entire political and military field, and every city strongly felt the Syracusan influence in its external and internal affairs.

It would be of great interest to know how the Sicels reacted in the first great conflict between Greeks and Carthaginians, but historical sources are mute in this respect, and archaeological evidence is lacking.

The indigenous population could hardly feel much sympathy for their Syracusan, Agrigentine, and Geloan overlords who certainly had treated them harshly. The tyrant dynasty of the Deinomenids were to them the very personification of oppression. But in the brief and decisive conflict of 480 B.C., the Sicels of the interior hardly had time to react. Hamilcar landed at Panormus and marched and sailed along the north coast the brief distance to Himera where he and his army met their fate. No crossing of the central parts of Sicily was called for, and no contacts between Hamilcar and the Sicels seem ever to have been established. This is the reason why none of the places in the Geloan or Agrigentine hinterland, studied by Adamesteanu, Orlandini, and De Miro, shows any traces of change in their interior development during these critical years. Our preliminary conclusion must, thus, be that the Greek tyrants in Syracuse, Gela, and Agrigentum held the Sicel situation firmly in hand.

But the time of the tyrants was running out. The two almost heroic figures of Gelon and Theron died in 478 and 472 B.C. Gelon's brother and successor, Hieron I, was short-lived, and after some internal strife between presumptive successors, the last of the great generation of tyrants ceased to exist in 466 B.C.

Syracuse, Agrigentum, and all the rest of the Sicilian cities went back to democratic rule, not without very serious difficulties.

During this new period in the history of Greek Sicily, the Sicels were, for the first time, participating actively in the affairs of the island. They did so not only because the new Greek governmental form gave everybody more free-dom of action than the old one had ever done, but also because they had amongst them an eminently talented and able man who could act as their leader. His name was Ducetius.

His appearance on the stage of the history is clearly conditioned by the confused situation in which Sicily, and above all Syracuse, found itself after the fall of the tyrants. Many delicate problems awaited solutions. The old landowners, driven away or transplanted by the autocratic Deinomenids, returned to their old homesteads and civil rights. A *modus vivendi* between them and the settlers brought in by the tyrants had to be found, and the thousands of mercenaries who had served the old masters had to be taken care of. All this could not take place without much strife and friction. It also meant a considerable weakening of Syracuse's military position, which was a *conditio sine qua non* for the success of Ducetius's plans.

In 461 B.C. most of the initial difficulties created by the newly acquired freedom were overcome. The only remaining stronghold of the Deinomenids was the city of Aetna-Inessa, a former Sicel center, Hellenized by Catane and taken over by Hieron I's youngest brother, Thrasyboulos, in 461 B.C. Here the last of the Deinomenids held forth, supported by the new Dorian settlers and an assorted crowd of mercenary soldiers.

When the new Syracusan regime moved against him, it received the effective help of Ducetius[2] and his Sicels, descending from their territory in the interior of the island close to present-day Mineo, Ducetius's birthplace. After having organized his fellow Sicels in a loose federation — a συντέλεια — in the new atmosphere of general freedom, his first action on the military and political scene was to side with the now democratic Syracuse against the remaining representative of the past tyranny. He did so on behalf of the town of Aetna-Inessa, situated on the southern slopes of Mount Etna. We know very little of its early history, and its location on the map is still debated,[3] but it must have had an early history similar to other Sicel centers in this region. Hellenized as a κτίσμα of Catane, its development probably followed the peaceful pattern of Chalcidian Hellenization and bi-racial coexistence. As was the case in Morgantina, this pattern was broken by the Geloan-Syracusan domination.

The action against Aetna-Inessa served, from a Syracusan point of view, to break the last Deinomenid resis-

Fig. 36. Destruction layer in a trench at Morgantina

Fig. 37. Burned houses in a trench at Morgantina

tance, and from Ducetius's standpoint it meant a vindication of the Sicel rights to freedom which had gained so much by the overthrow of the Deinomenids.

Thus, in the beginning of his erratic career, Ducetius sided with the Syracusan democracy. Diodorus (XI. 76) then calls him ὁ τῶν Σικελῶν ἡγεμών. His next move was decidedly not pro-Syracusan. From his base at Menainon he marched, in 459 B.C., against the city of Morgantina which, since the times of Hippocrates and Gelon, had belonged to the Deinomenid sphere of interest. We do not know the political affiliations of Morgantina at this time and cannot, therefore, guess Ducetius's motivation for attacking it. Archaeology does not tell us of such things. We can only assert that during the first half of the fifth century B.C. Morgantina continued to flourish as a Greek city. Diodorus (XI. 78) tells us that Morgantina was an important city (ἀξιόλογος πόλις), and that Ducetius — now called ὁ τῶν Σικελῶν βασιλεύς — took it by storm and gained much renown by this deed among his fellow Sicels.

For Morgantina the year 459 B.C. was a catastrophic date and marked the end of its first flourishing period. The results gained from the excavations speak a clear language.

Wherever a trench has been dug over the entire acropolis area, we have found traces of a thorough destruction datable to this time (Figs. 36, 37). Heavy layers of ashes and carbonized matter cover the built-up area. Burned roof timber and tumbled mudbrick walls form a thick deposit over the entire zone. As far as we can judge, not one house survived the catastrophe. The blow came suddenly. So heavy was the blow and so thorough was the destruction that more than one hundred and fifty years had to pass before life returned to the acropolis of Morgantina.

By the capture and destruction of Morgantina Ducetius eradicated a flourishing Greek city from his territory. In that sense his action was clearly anti-Greek and anti-Syracusan. It seems to contrast with his attitude two years earlier when he sided with the forces of the Syracusan democracy and helped to ferret out the last of the tyrants from Sicilian soil. If we have to consider Ducetius as a man following a clear political program — and this has been said lately with great emphasis[4] — we can hardly explain his brutal destruction of Morgantina, if we do not assume that it was dominated by forces, mercenary or otherwise, dedicated to the cause of the defunct tyrannical regime.

Ducetius's early sympathy for the ruling democrats in Syracuse can, however, not conceal that his main policy was anti-Greek, and pro-Sicel. He wanted to create, and partly succeeded in doing so, a confederation — a συντέλεια — of free Sicel cities with their respective territories. Such a confederation could have become a third power in Sicily and changed much of the island's history had it survived its creator.

Adamesteanu has rightly pointed out that the methods Ducetius followed in his attempts were really closely based on those he so vigorously opposed, i.e., those practiced by the tyrants of the past generation. He founded a national Sicel shrine at Palice, near Mineo, kept and strengthened the fortresses of the inland region — τὰ φρούρια τῶν Σικελῶν — and destroyed ruthlessly those he considered his enemies. In this sense, he was profoundly Hellenized.

His political shrewdness and wisdom made it possible for him to hold his own even when the political and military power of the two new democracies, Syracuse and Agrigentum, increased and again became consolidated. He maneuvered in such a way that Syracuse and Agrigentum found no reason to join against him. His conquests of the Greco-Siculan centers on ex-Chalcidian territory were exclusively to the damage of Syracuse.

But in 452 B.C. he reached also into the Agrigentine hinterland and conquered one of their strongest fortress towns, Motyon, on the upper Salso River. Adamesteanu has offered arguments for identifying it with the present-day Vassallaggio.[5] If that is correct, we obtain at least some lead in judging the topographical setting of Ducetius's last fight as ὁ βασιλεύς τῶν Σικελῶν. The first battle between him and the joint Greek forces ended in a Sicel victory, but the campaign of 450 B.C. became decisive. Ducetius was beaten and his forces were dispersed.

So the war of national resistance ended and the episode of Ducetius came to an end.

Strangely enough, he gave himself up to the Syracusans who, in spite of Agrigentine protests, magnanimously spared him and allowed him to go into exile to their own mother city, Corinth.

It is not easy to draw any wide conclusion on Ducetius's activity and his rôle in Sicilian history. It was spurred by a strong hatred of the past Syracusan and Agrigentine regimes of suppression and domination. In that sense it was built up on an ideal of obtaining freedom for the Sicels, while saving the benefits of Hellenic civilization as it thrived in the πόλεις, κτίσματα and πολισμάτια in central Sicily. In that sense it was a policy of cooperation with the Hellenic secondary colonists. His early enterprise in favor of Aetna-Inessa was indirectly a benefit to the Chalcidian Catanaeans, who, in their early colonial days, had championed the same idea of cooperation and coexistence between Sicels and Greeks. This ideal, rather than uncompromising nationalism, may ultimately and originally have been the driving force of the Sicel leader. His confederation of Sicel sites in central Sicily seems to have been created to obtain for his people a cooperation on equal terms by negotiating from strength. The main obstacle to its realization was certainly the mightiest power of Sicily, Syracuse, which finally brought about his fall.

The resilience and the diplomatic talents of Ducetius, which saved his life in 450 B.C., were again demonstrated in the last years of his life. In 446 B.C. he surprisingly returned from exile to his native island, this time as leader of a colonial enterprise, participants in which came mostly from Corinth itself. From having been the first political and military leader of the Sicels, he became one of the last of the colonial leaders of the Greeks in Sicily. As a settlement he chose Caleacte on the north coast, far from his own early foundations of Palice and Menainon. The region is poor and had been neglected by the early Greek settlers. The Nebrodian mountains look down on a narrow strip of land which offers only poor agricultural prospects. The motivation for his choice is difficult to understand. Adamesteanu[6] may be right when he suggests that Ducetius's reasons were well calculated. He knew already that the central parts of the island were so firmly in Syracusan and Agrigentine hands that any attempt to reestablish himself there would have been hopeless. Caleacte on the north coast would at least serve as an obstacle to further Syracusan expansion in this direction, and, at the same time, could become the core of a new region where Greco-Sicel cooperation would be practiced. Whatever his long-range policy and plans may have been, they were cut short by his death in 440 B.C. With his disappearance from the stage, the curtain fell on the strange and fascinating play in which he had been the only actor.

The archaeological picture, illustrating the events during the two decades of Ducetius's operations, is as shifting and unpredictable as the military and political actions of the Sicel leader. We have already seen that the settlement on the acropolis of Morgantina was so thoroughly destroyed that life did not return there until the end of the fourth century.

Still further inland in the region of Agrigentine penetration lies Sabucina quite close to present-day Caltanisetta, lately excavated by Orlandini.[7] A strong Greek φρούριον, dating from the late sixth century B.C. with the usual set-up of houses and sanctuaries, flourished on the site until the beginning of the Ducetian rebellion, around 460. Then it was destroyed by violent action, probably to be attributed to Ducetius. Unlike Morgantina, however, there are several signs of continued life in Sabucina during the latter half of the fifth century.[8]

On the neighboring sites of Vassallaggio[9] and Gibil Gabib,[10] no destruction can be traced at all during the same period. Settlements and cemeteries give an unbroken series of finds through the fifth century.

The only conclusion which suggests itself under these circumstances is that the many settlements in the interior underwent different treatment because of their different behavior during these critical years. Some of them, such as Vassallaggio, may have opened their gates to Ducetius's forces and cooperated with him. Others, like Morgantina, put up a decisive defense and succumbed to the conqueror with devastating consequences for the city. Others again, like Gibil Gabib, may have been able to resist the attacks and to continue their lives more or less undisturbed. The φρούρια may also have remained neutral or shifted allegiance during the critical years and thus succeeded in avoiding the hostilities of the two fighting parties.

This warns us that the Ducetius movement was not in any way a monolithic anti-Greek uprising, as it is often described. Ancient historical texts and archaeological evidence seem to concur in painting a much more varied and complicated picture of these dramatic events.

During these critical decades we hear nothing of the Carthaginians in Sicily. If they had nourished any thought of revenge for their defeat at Himera in 480 B.C., there would have been more than one occasion which would have looked propitious for realizing such plans. They never moved to side with Ducetius in his wars with Syracuse and Agrigentum, nor did they grasp the opportunity when Syracuse was weakened by internal strife after the fall of the Deinomenids. Possibly the terrible experience of 480 was still present in their minds and made them hesitant to embark on a similar enterprise. No source indicates that Ducetius ever sought their help even when he was in the depths of distress. So Hellenic was this anti-Greek leader that he preferred to throw himself at the mercy of the Syracusans than to call in the barbarians from the west.

The truth seems to be that Carthage, during these years, was quietly building up her power position in Africa and, therefore, refraining from any intervention policy overseas.[11] Carthage was not even moved to intervene when her old ally in Sicily, the Elymian city of Segesta, directly appealed to her for help in a border conflict with Selinus in 458 B.C.[12]

Instead of Carthage, it was Athens who signed a treaty of friendship and support with Segesta.[13] This was Athenian expansion policy at work for the first time in the West. Pericles' interest in the world of the Western Greeks is manifest also in the foundation of the new colony of Thurii in Calabria in 443, and in the treaty of friendship of 433 with Rhegium and Leontini, two Chalcidian colonies which both felt the pressure of Syracusan power expansion.

We know of Syracusan armaments on a grand scale in the years after the fall of Ducetius. The navy was brought up to one hundred trireme ships, the cavalry forces were doubled and the infantry better equipped: "This," says Diodorus (XII. 30.1), "they were doing with the intention of subduing all Sicily little by little."

No wonder that the non-Dorian Greeks in Sicily began looking for support from the mightiest power in the mother country.

This is not the place to follow the story of Athenian intervention in Sicily from its hesitant beginnings in 427 to its catastrophic end in 413 B.C. An attempt will be made only to investigate the rôle played by the Sicels in the fight of the two great powers. Thucydides is our source, supplemented here and there by Diodorus.

Athens seems to have counted on the support of the Sicels in the fight against Syracuse. At least such help was one of the arguments Alcibiades presented to the assembly in Athens when he recommended the Sicilian expedition in 416 B.C. (VI. 17): "We shall have the help of many barbarians who from hatred of the Syracusans will join us in attacking them."

Hermocrates, on the other side, warning the Syracusans of the impending attack, had evidently the same presentiment, as he strongly advised his fellow citizens to obtain the friendship of the Sicels, who might prove valuable allies (VI. 34).

After the Athenian landing in Himera, Nicias, their commander-in-chief, sailed along the north coast "to their Sicel allies to urge them to send troops." The "Sicel allies" along the north coast could be none else than the Caleacteans, Ducetius's colonists of 446 B.C. It is interesting to see that Ducetius's old traditional anti-Syracusan policy still was adhered to by his successors (VI. 63). Some of the Sicels joined the Athenian forces and sailed on board the fleet to Syracuse (VI. 65). These barbarian allies of Athens "owed most of their ardor to the desire of self-preservation ($\sigma\omega\tau\eta\rho\acute{\iota}\alpha$) which they could only hope for if victorious. Next to which, as a secondary motive, came the chance of serving on easier terms, after helping the Athenians to a new conquest." (VI. 69)

During the winter, when the Athenians were encamped in Naxos, negotiations were again opened with the Sicels. Those in the neighborhood of the Plain, "as subjects of Syracuse, mostly held aloof, but the peoples of the interior who had never been otherwise than independent, with few exceptions, at once joined the Athenians, and brought corn to the army, in some cases even money" (VI. 88). One would like to believe that Morgantina, which was no longer a Syracusan dependency after the Congress of Gela in 424 B.C., was one of the contributors to this anti-Syracusan effort. We hear also (ibid.) that the Athenians even tried to enroll Sicel allies by force, marching against those who hesitated to join.

In the first year of the war Athenian propaganda, combined with some more forceful arguments of persuasion, obviously was successful in swinging the Sicel public opinion to their favor. They championed, after all, the case of their Chalcidian allies who had always been on better terms with the indigenous populations than had the Dorians, particularly under the Deinomenids.

In the following spring of 415 B.C. the Athenians took by capitulation the city of Centuripe between Morgantina and the coast, and they burned the corn of Inessa and Hybla. The two latter towns were situated on the lowest slopes of Mount Etna, close to the Catania Plain. The Athenian action could have been motivated only by the fact that these cities were in the Syracusan fold, their geographic position forcing them to remain there. They were waiting on the sidelines to see how the military situation developed. After the initial tactical successes of the Athenian forces outside Syracuse, Thucydides tells us that "many of the Sicels who had hitherto been looking to see how things went, came as allies to the Athenians" (VI. 103). Earlier in the summer, "a hundred cavalrymen from Sicels, Naxians, and others" had already taken the Athenian side (VI. 98).

From 414 B.C. and onward, after the arrival of the Spartan general, Gylippus, and his reinforcements for the Syracusan army, the situation began to change in the same rhythm as the Athenian prestige sank. As early as at his landing in Himera, Gylippus obtained a "few troops from the Sicels (VII. 1) and after the death of Archonidas of Herbita, the Sicels joined Gylippus with more alacrity." This is symptomatic, because with Archonidas died the remnants of the spirit and political principles of Ducetius.

At that moment, the tide turned. Nicias's letter to Athens, written in the early fall, tells the sad story of Sicel deserters with much sincerity: "Such of them who were pressed into service take the first opportunity of departing to their respective cities; such as were originally seduced by the temptation of high pay, and expected little fighting and large gains, leave us either by desertion to the enemy or by availing themselves of one or other of the various facilities of escape which the magnitude of Sicily affords them," (VII. 13).

But even when things looked really bad, some Sicels stuck to the Athenian cause and did their best to block the way of auxiliary troops on their way through the interior to Syracuse. Centuripe, a neighboring town of Morgantina's, was among the cities which did so (VII. 32).

When Thucydides, at the end of his story of the final Athenian catastrophe, presents a list of Athenian allies, he includes "most of the Sicels" (VII. 57), while on the Syracusan side were "of the barbarians, the Sicels, that is to say, only those who did not go over to the Athenians"

(VII. 58).

Such is Thucydides' record, scrutinized page by page. For all of us who know Thucydides as a historian, it is no surprise that his information on our specific topic is somewhat scanty. He belongs to those authors who stick rigidly to their topic, "the war between the Peloponnesians and the Athenians," as he defines it in the first sentence of his first book. He does not allow himself to be distracted by details which have not a strict and close bearing "on this war of which Thucydides is the historian," as he often repeats it.

Although the material is not abundant, I would consider it sufficient for a somewhat general synthesis of the rôle of the Sicels during the period of time it covers.[14]

The Athenians were right in counting on the sympathy and help of the indigenous populations of Sicily in their great Syracusan war. Alcibiades was correctly informed when he held out that possibility to the Athenian assembly at the beginning of the expedition. What he might not have known was that these feelings of the Sicels had deep roots and a wide historical background. Athens fought, nominally at least, on the side of the Chalcidian colonies of the east coast which had, since the days of the colonization, kept rapport with the indigenous populations. Their open κτίσματα in the interior contrasted favorably to the Dorian φρούρια and the Syracusan subcolonies where the Sicels remained a suppressed and enslaved group of non-citizens.

Ducetius understood this and gave it a stamp of national policy that no other Sicel had ever been able to do, although his political career may seem both erratic and opportunistic. His legacy to his Hellenized compatriots, whom Thucydides never hesitates to call βάρβαροι, was basically pro-Ionian democratic and anti-Dorian autocratic. A sufficient remnant of this legacy was still a living reality at the time of the great conflict and functioned as the main motivation for the ready help the Sicels gave the Athenians and their Chalcidian allies in Sicily.

The year 413 B.C. is an important date in the history of Sicily. It signifies a conclusion, not only for Athenian ambitions, but also for the hopes of their Chalcidian allies to live their independent lives as freely operating Greek city states. The war of 416–413 B.C. ended in such an overwhelming Syracusan triumph that Syracuse virtually became the master of Sicilian affairs. Its power and influence was felt everywhere in the island, with the possible exception of the northwestern region which was dominated by the Carthaginians.

For the student of ancient Sicilian history who works with this period, the year 413 also means a farewell to the best and most reliable source for the reconstruction of the events, that is, to Thucydides, whose orderly and precise narration means so much for the illumination of our theme. For the events of the last decade of the fifth century and the entire fourth century we are referred to Diodorus Siculus and to Plutarch, the former a compiler of questionable reliability and the latter a moralizing biographer. The difference between the critical eyewitness and the secondhand narrators is enormous, and we have to expect a comparable difference between the preceding results of our inquiry and those relating to this later period.

It was a border conflict between Selinus and Segesta which triggered the first Athenian intervention in Sicily in 458 B.C. The same seemingly peripheral and unimportant reason was the ultimate cause of the catastrophic events of 410 B.C. and the subsequent years.

For the sequence of events, Diodorus (XIII. 43 ff.) is our only source. When the Selinuntines invaded Segestan territory and pretended to occupy it for good, the Segestans countered by sending an embassy to Carthage asking for help. It must be said that the Carthaginians behaved in a very considerate manner. Their respect for the might of Syracuse was so deep that they preferred to refer the dispute to Syracuse for arbitration, a proposition rejected by Selinus. Syracuse seemed relieved not to be directly involved in the conflict and kept her old alliance with Selinus without breaking the peace with Carthage.

The Carthaginian leader was Hannibal the Elder, grandson of the Hamilcar who had suffered the crushing defeat at Himera in his war with Gelon in 480 B.C. He first sent a small mercenary force to assist Segesta. It effectively beat off the Selinuntines who then, applying directly to Syracuse for help, received promises of assistance. "And so," says Diodorus (XIII. 44.5), "the Carthaginian war had its beginning."

Hannibal came well prepared. He landed with his numerous troops in Lilybaeum, present-day Marsala, and from there he marched southward to Selinus and the siege began. The defense was heroic, but no help arrived in time from Syracuse, Agrigentum, or Gela. After nine days the city fell into Hannibal's hands, in 409 B.C. Its fate was frightful. Sixteen thousand citizens, men, women, and children, were killed, five thousand were taken prisoner, and the town was burned and plundered. Only twenty-six hundred survivors made their way to Agrigentum. This was certainly the hardest blow ever dealt to Hellenism in Sicily, but there was more to come.

Hannibal remembered his grandfather's defeat and death at Himera seventy years earlier and set out to take his revenge. Himera met a fate still more terrible than Selinus. "Thus, Hannibal in the course of three months captured two Greek cities, Selinus and Himera," Xenophon summarizes the events (*Hell.* I. 1.37). He marched his forces inland, through Agrigentine territory, probably up the Halykos River valley toward the north coast. During the crossing his army was joined by twenty thousand Sicels and Sicans (Diod. XIII. 59.6).

This information is of some interest. The indigenous populations in the distant hinterland of Agrigentum and Gela had become Hellenized by the establishment of a great number of Greek fortified settlements ($\phi\rho o\acute{v}\rho\iota\alpha$) and small towns ($\pi o\lambda\acute{\iota}\chi\nu\iota\alpha$) during the second half of the sixth century B.C. We know many of them, thanks to the archaeological explorations of Griffo, Adamesteanu, Orlandini, and De Miro in the towns of Sabucina,[15] Vassallaggio,[16] Gibil Gabib,[17] Capo d'Arso,[18] and others. Their Hellenization, however, obviously had not made the indigenous Sicans and Sicels of this region into political Philhellenes. We have traced earlier the oppressive and authoritarian policy which characterized the establishment of secondary colonies by the Dorian cities on the south coast.

Hannibal the Elder, who was not only a great military leader but also an accomplished diplomat, had apparently appealed to the patriotic feelings of the indigenous tribes with resounding success. The older generation still remembered Ducetius, and the Sicans and Sicels alike found in Hannibal a new and powerful leader against the ruling Dorian Greeks. Some of these settlements, particularly the Greek fortresses, may well have opposed the Carthaginian "liberator" and were taken by force and destroyed during this critical period.[19] Vassallaggio and Sabucina may have belonged to this group. Both seem to show an interval in their flourishing civic lives, beginning

with the end of the fifth century. However, we need more systematic research on the other sites in this region before we are able to give a more specific picture of the repercussions of these decisive events on the political attitude of the indigenous populations.

After a lull of a couple of years and an uneasy truce, embassies were exchanged between Carthage and Syracuse, but the negotiations were of no avail and the war broke out again. Hannibal gathered another large army and a powerful navy. This time, Syracuse, which had failed to bring help in time to Selinus three years earlier, tried to organize a common defense against the invading barbarians. She engaged the forces of some of the Greek cities in Magna Graecia as well.

Agrigentum was the immediate target of the Carthaginian forces, and it fell to Hannibal after a prolonged siege, in spite of some well-intended but belated Syracusan action and some help received also from Greece proper. Before the city fell in December, 406 B.C., part of its population was evacuated to Gela (Diod. XIII. 89.3). The fall of Agrigentum was a calamity to the Hellenic cause in Sicily equal in magnitude to the loss of Selinus and Himera.

Under these intensely dramatic and critical circumstances, there rose to power in Syracuse a young, highly talented, and much debated character, the son-in-law of Hermocrates and future tyrant of Syracuse, Dionysius I. Meanwhile, the Carthaginian advance along the south coast continued unabated and soon also Gela and Camarina were in barbaric hands. Himilco, the successor of Hannibal the Elder who had fallen at the capture of Agrigentum, was outside the walls of Syracuse itself. The city was saved thanks mostly to a plague which carried away half of the Carthaginian forces (Diod. XIII. Table of Contents, last paragraph). A peace treaty was signed between the two belligerent parties in 405 B.C.

This treaty was disastrous to the Greeks. The Carthaginian $\dot{\epsilon}\pi\iota\kappa\rho\acute{a}\tau\epsilon\iota\alpha$, or dominion, was to include the entire Elymian region around Segesta and the Sican territories in the west: Selinus, Himera, Agrigentum, Gela, and Camarina would remain Greek but pay tribute to the Carthaginians and leave their cities unfortified. Syracuse had to give up its hegemony over Messana and Leontini and "let the Sicels remain autonomous" (Diod. XIII. 114.1). Finally, Cathage guaranteed Dionysius's power position in Syracuse.

The paragraph concerning the Sicels must have been particularly humiliating to Syracuse, which only ten years earlier had established its power over the indigenous populations of the east and central region of the island. We are not informed as to how the Syracusan overlordship of the cities of the interior manifested itself, but in most cases it probably consisted in the keeping of a garrison. If the peace treaty abolished the dishonorable burden, Carthage had certainly acquired considerable good will among the Sicels. We are equally ignorant concerning the meaning of the phrase, Σικελοὺς ἅπαντας αὐτονόμους εἶναι. Literally it means "to have their own laws," but what such a constitutional condition indicates is not quite clear.

Later on in the fourth century we meet several independent Sicel cities governed by completely Hellenized petty princes or chieftains, and it seems most probable that the autonomy of the Sicel towns, guaranteed by Carthage, took this form of government as early as at the end of the fifth century. (Cf. below, p. 59)

That Dionysius resented the freedom given to the Sicels was in accordance with old Syracusan tradition. For, as we have seen, oppression of the indigenous populations seems to have belonged to Syracusan tradition, right from the beginning of the first contacts between the two ethnic elements in the eighth and seventh centuries B.C.

Not more than one year passed after the signature of the treaty between Carthage and Dionysius until the latter broke the paragraph referring to the independence of the Sicels. Diodorus (XIV. 7.5–6) tells us, "when Dionysius thought that he had now organized his tyranny properly, he led forth his army against the Sicels, being eager to bring all the independent peoples under his control, and the Sicels in particular, because of their previous alliance with the Carthaginians. Accordingly he advanced against the city of Herbessus and made preparations for its siege." It is uncertain where Herbessus was situated, but it is generally assumed that it was not very far from Syracuse, possibly at the present village of Buscemi.

These operations were interrupted by a mutiny in Syracuse against the tyrant, but Dionysius succeeded in quelling the uprising.

The subsequent year, 403 B.C., brought more dramatic events and allowed Dionysius to fortify his position as absolute ruler of Syracuse.

He appeared before Leontini and captured Catane in a rapid sequence of events. He made his presence felt also as far inland as in Enna. This means that he had crossed through the very core of Sicel territory. In these contexts, he made an assault on Herbita, a Greco-Siculan mountain town, possibly to be identified with present-day Troina. All these operations seem to have had as one of their motives the plan to vindicate his overlordship, his superiority over what Diodorus calls οἱ Σικελοί, who, as we now know, really were a mixture of Greeks and thoroughly Hellenized Sicels. As a gesture of conciliation toward these elements whose freedom was guaranteed by the treaty of 405 B.C., we may possibly interpret his handing over the territory of Naxos to them (Diod. XIV. 15.3). With equally lavish generosity, he gave the city of Catane to his Campanian mercenaries (ibid.), thus eliminating the two oldest of the Chalcidian colonies on the island.

Dionysius had not left much of the substance of his peace treaty with Carthage unviolated, but still peace was formally maintained. We learn with some surprise that "no small number of Carthaginians had their homes in Syracuse and rich possessions, and many also of their merchants had vessels in the harbor, loaded with goods . . ." (Diod. XIV, 46.1). Such a coexistence between Greeks and Carthaginians was not limited to Syracuse alone, but seems at that time to have been the rule in all the Siceliot cities (Diod. XIV. 46.2). These Carthaginians became, of course, the first victims when, in 398 B.C., Dionysius sent an embassy to Carthage with the short message: "The Syracusans declare war upon the Carthaginians unless they restore freedom to the Greek cities that they have enslaved" (Diod. XIV. 46.5). So, Dionysius's first Carthaginian war broke out in 397 B.C. and lasted for a little more than one year. It carried Dionysius victorious wherever he went, and his military marches were long and swiftly carried out. Camarina, Gela, and Agrigentum were liberated first; the old Carthaginian stronghold of Motya was captured and destroyed. The great mobility of the armies in this war is a specific feature which tells us of organized logistics and good military roads.

Another characteristic of particular interest to our theme is the obvious attempt made by both belligerent parties to engage the sympathies and help of the indigenous populations. We learn from Diodorus (XIV. 48.4) that, after the liberation of Agrigentum, Sican towns joined Dionysius's forces. These towns must be the same that we have heard of before, situated in the Sican hinterland up the valleys of the rivers Salso and Platani, and which had fallen into Carthaginian hands in 405 B.C.

When Motya fell, Dionysius garrisoned the ruined city with Sicel forces (Diod. XIV. 53.5) under Syracusan command.

A counter offensive was launched by the Carthaginians which carried them right to Messana. During the advance their leader, Himilco, took up friendly relations with the Sicels in Cephaloedium and in the territory of Himera (Diod. XIV. 56.2). He crowned this year of 397 by the eminently pro-Sicel gesture of founding the town of Tauromenium and giving it to the Sicels (Diod. XIV. 59.1).

In the same year we hear from Diodorus (XIV. 58.1): "The Sicels who had hated Dionysius from of old and now had an opportunity to revolt went over in a body, with the exception of the people of Assorus, to the Carthaginians." This must have been a serious blow to Dionysius's strategic and political plans. It shows the importance both fighting parties attributed to the support they could obtain from the Hellenized Sicels, and it demonstrates equally well the opportunistic way in which the Sicels availed themselves of the shifting situations created by the changing success of the war. We know from numerous archaeological arguments that, from a cultural point of view, they were fully and thoroughly Hellenized. Solidarity with the Greek cause against the alien barbarians did not, however, follow the cultural ties. In this field, their main goal was to safeguard their own municipal freedom and political independence as best they could. Their long experience, dating back to the time of Ducetius, told them that a strong Syracuse under royal-tyrannical rule yielded little chance of realizing such ambitions and hopes. Therefore, they always seemed ready to join any anti-Syracusan coalition which appeared on the military or political stage and which seemed to have any hope of success. No wonder then that, after the military success of Himilco in 396 B.C. which brought him to the gates of Syracuse, the Sicels were eager to join him. But luck shifted again, and before the end of the year the Carthaginian forces, both army and navy, which besieged Syracuse were thoroughly routed. This unexpected turn naturally placed the Sicel allies of Himilco in a very critical situation. "The Sicels who were serving in the army of the Carthaginians forestalling the Syracusans fled

through the interior and, almost to a man, made their way in safety to their native home" (Diod. XIV, 75.6).

Under the circumstances, it does not surprise us that Dionysius, after having concluded a peace treaty with Carthage, undertook a series of severe actions which basically must be understood as directed toward obtaining a firmer grip on the Sicels.

The Sicel territory of Abacaenum to the east of Messana was split up, and Dionysius founded a new sub-colony at Tyndaris (Diod. XIV. 78.5). He moved populations in a radical way. The former Naxians, who were a hapless lot, were again exiled from Mylae where they had settled under Rhegian protection (Diod. XIV. 87.3), and subsequently dispersed. Typically enough, some of them took refuge and settled in Sicel cities, a fact that again reminds us of the friendly relations that of old had existed between the Chalcidian colonists and the Sicels (*ibid.*). This happened, according to Diodorus, in the year 394 B.C.

Two years earlier, in 396 B.C., "Dionysius waged a number of campaigns against the territory of the Sicels, in the course of which he took Menaenum and Morgantina and struck a treaty with Agyris, the tyrant of the Agyrinaeans, and Damon, the lord of the Centuripans, as well as with the Herbitaeans and people of Assorus. He also gained by treachery Cephaloedium, Solocis and Enna, and made peace besides with the Herbessians" (Diod. XIV. 78.7).

A few comments on this important passage are in order. Dionysius struck at the heart of the Sicel country and concentrated his efforts on subduing those Hellenized Sicel centers that belonged originally to the Chalcidian settlements, where Ducetius in the middle of the fifth century had built up his territorial power. Menaenum was his birthplace; Morgantina was his first conquest which was lost by Syracuse to Camarina after the Congress of Gela in 424 B.C. (Thucydides IV. 65.1) Assorus and Agyrium are its two closest neighboring cities. Centuripe lies in the same region and Herbita, although not yet safely identified, was probably located where the present-day town of Troina lies. Enna, "umbilicus Siciliae," is still further inland. All of these cities had lived autonomously after the peace treaty of 405 B.C. and were governed by Hellenized local chieftains. Dionysius's re-conquest put an end to this relative freedom in most of the cases which Diodorus enumerates. It is of some importance to note that Dionysius's drive brought him to the north coast. Together with the foundation of Tyndaris, this move put a definite end to the dream of Ducetius, whose foundation of Caleacte in 446 B.C. seems to have been aimed as a brake on further Syracusan advances in this direction.

Dionysius was unsuccessful only in one enterprise in this anti-Sicel war, and that was his failure to capture Tauromenium (Diod. XIV. 88), the town that Himilco had founded and given to the Sicels in 397 B.C.

The second Carthaginian war of Dionysius broke out in 392 B.C. This time the Carthaginians took the initiative, first on the diplomatic level. Their general, Mago, "set about retrieving the Carthaginian cause after the disaster they had suffered, for he showed kindness to the subject cities and received the victims of Dionysius's wars. He also founded alliances with most of the Sicels" (Diod. XIV. 90.3).

Carthaginian action seems to follow a now well-known pattern. The war itself was less dramatic. Mago set out from Panormus along the north coast, as he was aiming to capture Messana, the key to the Straits. Abacaenum, the old Sicel town east of Messana, became one of his allies and served as his headquarters during part of the operations. Thereafter, he turned to the Sicel cities of the interior (Diod. XIV. 95) and succeeded in persuading most of them to sever their bonds with Dionysius. However, Agyrium, which might at this time have been the direct political overlord of Morgantina, held on to their old alliance. As these events were occurring, Dionysius himself started out from Syracuse. Without any decisive battle ever taking place, negotiations for peace were begun, and before the end of the year the treaty was signed. The conditions maintained the status quo, except for two paragraphs, both relating to the Sicels: 1) Dionysius should be their lord; 2) he should receive Tauromenium which he had failed to take earlier by force (Diod. XIV. 96.4). This peace treaty seems to have ended Sicel resistance against Dionysius for good.

The Syracusan tyrant-king was free to dedicate his energies and talents toward the creation of his south-Italian and Adriatic empire. This empire was one of the more remarkable achievements in the history of the Greek world before the conquests of Alexander the Great.

In 383 B.C. the third Carthaginian war broke out. It was fought with varying success, mostly in Dionysius's new territories in south Italy, and came to an end after a couple of years (Diod. XV. 15–17) with small change in the conditions established by the earlier treaty.

Once again, however, Dionysius returned to his Carthaginian warfare. In 368 B.C. he started operations on a grand scale, following a pattern very much like that of his first Carthaginian war. Selinus was reconquered and Eryx with its new harbor, Drepanon (Trapani), were taken, but his navy suffered a serious setback in the process (Diod. XV. 73.3–4). Before the year's war season was over, however, Dionysius died. He had ruled for thirty-eight years, and was succeeded by his son, Dionysius II.

We have no reason to follow the confused history of Syracuse during the reign of Dionysius II, nor the rivalries and court intrigues which filled the years between 367 and 345 B.C. Syracusan power ($\dot{\alpha}\rho\chi\dot{\eta}$) over the Sicel territory was well-established and controlled by military commanders ($\phi\rho o\acute{\upsilon}\rho\alpha\rho\chi o\iota$) stationed in most of the important cities of the interior. Treaty-bound alliances were established with the $\pi\acute{o}\lambda\epsilon\iota\varsigma$ Ἑλληνίδες of Agrigentum, Gela, Camarina, Thermae Himeraeae, and with the cities of Tyndaris, Agyrium, Centuripe, Herbita, Assorus, and the Megalo-Hellenic Locri (Diod. XIV. 78). Under these circumstances, firm Syracusan control prevented Carthaginian intervention.

From a Hellenic point of view, however, things were far from satisfactory. A major and permanent problem was created by the presence in Sicily of the mercenary troops supported by Dionysius II. They were neither Sicels nor Greeks, but rather mostly alien barbarians from Spain and Campania. They were the props of his power and played a great role in Sicilian internal affairs of the period.

Dionysius II, like his father, was interested in literature and philosophy, and invited Plato and a numerous group of leading philosophers to his court. Plato visited him twice, in 365 and in 361 B.C. In one of the letters that falsely go under Plato's name (Letter VIII), the problem of the mercenaries is particularly discussed. If the problem is not solved, the author, who has an intimate knowledge of Sicilian affairs, foresees that the horrible but inevitable consequence will be "the extinction of Greek language in the whole of Sicily, and the transformation of the Siceliote culture into a Phoenician and Campanian province" (VIII. 353. E). Through a continuous infiltration of non-Hellenized and powerful groups of Iberians and Campanians, who as veterans were settled in different towns, Sicily was menaced by de-Hellenization, at least as far as the spoken language was concerned.

In 345 B.C. Dionysius II resided for some time in Locri in Italy, and the Syracusans used the occasion to try to bring about a betterment of their domestic situation. Their method was traditional. They sent to their mother city, Corinth, an embassy to ask for an able and honest leader who could deliver them from tyranny, as well as from all the evils that followed this form of government. The Corinthians consented, and their choice was excellent: Timoleon, a firm believer in the democratic form of government, a refined diplomat, and a very competent military leader. With his arrival in Sicily begins a new era in the history of the island, properly known as the Timoleontic revival.

This period has recently been the object of penetrating studies. The entire fourth volume of the review *Kokalos* (1958) is dedicated to this topic. A general reference to that collection of articles may suffice for the argumentation from case to case.

Timoleon's mission was eminently well fulfilled. Not only did Timoleon beat the Carthaginians in the great battle of Krimisos in 339 B.C., but still more important, he succeeded in establishing a firm democratic rule in Syracuse. The Sicels followed an old pattern in their subsequent behavior. No sooner had they obtained guarantees of a relative independence and of municipal self-government from the new and well-entrenched democratic party in Syracuse than their pro-Carthaginian feelings dissipated. The Sicel cities joined Timoleon with enthusiasm and success in his anti-Carthaginian war.

Timoleon's general policy brought Sicily back on her feet remarkably soon. Wherever archaeological investigations have been undertaken, there is abundant proof of great material progress in this period — from Gela and Heraclea Minoa on the south coast to Tyndaris and Lipari in the north.[20] All over the interior territory of central Sicily, cities and settlements were rebuilt, currency circulation became abundant, and independent farms were scattered over the country side. The resiliency of Sicily in this period is quite astounding. A few years of peace and decent government were all that were needed to bring back the general prosperity of the intrinsically wealthy island. Diodorus (XVI. 83.1) says about Timoleon: ἐποίησε τὰς πόλεις ταχὺ λαβεῖν πολλὴν αὔξησιν πρὸς εὐδαιμονίαν, and his words are fully borne out by the archaeological evidence.

One of Timoleon's most important accomplishments was to organize the free cities, both the old coastal colonies and the towns of the interior, into a free federation, a συμμαχία, the members of which kept enough of their sovereignty to strike their own bronze coinage. He drove out the remaining tyrants from the Sicel cities and destroyed or confined the loose mercenary troops (Diod. XVI. 82.4–5). All the foundations for a rebirth of Sicily were laid by this formidable organizer and great statesman.

Still, the ravages of the past had left great gaps in the ranks of the Greek population, both Siceliote and Sicel. Timoleon saw the necessity of a recolonization on a large scale and carried it through with great foresight and with far-reaching consequences. His heralds were sent to Greece and the islands and invited new settlers on generous terms. Forty thousand were welcomed and settled on Syracusan lands; Agyrium in the interior received another ten thousand (Diod. XVI. 82.5).

This giant operation saved the Hellenism of Sicily and effected a long-lasting reconciliation between the indigenous populations and the Greek colonists of the island.

6 *Greek Civilization in Sicily*

There are some good reasons for asking whether the problem implicit in the title of this chapter, *Greek Civilization in Sicily,* is a topic capable of a valid analysis.[1]

Was there really any intrinsic difference between the Greek culture of the motherland and of Sicily?[2] The colonists of the west brought with them on arrival a genuinely Greek civilization, and they never lost contact with their mother cities and their entire homeland. They participated in the Panhellenic festivals of Delphi, Olympia, Isthmus, and Nemea with enthusiasm and success. Pindar and Simonides celebrated in their odes the victories of Syracusans, Agrigentines, and Camarinaeans,[3] and Aeschylus visited the island where his tragedies were played in the theater of Syracuse.[4] Among the monuments and treasuries in Delphi and Olympia, those erected by Sicilian Greeks were of equal, if not superior, quality to those of their fellow countrymen of continental and insular Greece.

Therefore, under these circumstances, the question whether there really existed a specific Greek civilization in Sicily is certainly legitimate.

It would be interesting to know what the Hellenes themselves of the mother country thought of the Siceliotes. Did they feel that there existed essential differences between them and real Greeks? We have, to my knowledge, only one testimony in that respect, and that is certainly biased. This is what Alcibiades said when he addressed the Athenian public assembly in 416 B.C., before the start of the Sicilian expedition: "Do not rescind your resolution to sail to Sicily on the grounds that you were going to attack a great power. Although the cities of Sicily are populous, the inhabitants are a mixed crowd and easily change their institutions and adopt new ones in their stead. No one really feels that he has a hometown of his own. They are badly provided with personal armaments and the country lacks an organized defence. Every man thinks that either by fair words or by party strife he can obtain something at the public expense, and then in the event of a catastrophe settle in some other country, and makes his preparations accordingly. From a mob like this you need not look for either unanimity in counsel or concert in action" (Thucy. VI. 17.2–4).

Alcibiades' contempt may have been sincere, but it should be remembered that his oration was held with the aim of persuading the assembly hesitant to follow him in the conquest of Sicily. Many of the reproaches which he directed at the Siceliotes could with equal justification have been addressed to the Athenians themselves or to any other group of Greeks of the mother country. It is interesting, however, to note that he accuses them of instability not only of mind, but also with regard to their dwelling places. The big cities of Sicily, and first of all Syracuse, were populated by mixed crowds. The heterogeneous composition of the population to which new citizens – ἔποικοι – could easily be added was a fact Alcibiades particularly pointed out. The territories – χῶραι – were vast and allowed a great mobility of the masses fundamentally unknown to the citizens of the more stable πόλεις of Greece proper. Wide space and fluid masses, two interdependent factors, were characteristics of the Greek civilization in Sicily. There Alcibiades was right. Whether this was a weakness, as he wanted his fellow Athenians to believe, or not, is certainly another question. It is a phenomenon met with in every colonial society where the flow of immigrants is constant. In many cases a society so constructed gains in dynamism what it loses in stability. This was proved by the Siceliotes, as it is today by the United States.

A comparison between the social and political structure of the big cities in Sicily and those of Greece proper can to some extent illustrate the problem. The presence of tyrants, which lasted in Sicily until about 460 B.C., is partially to be explained by the rigid social stratigraphy of the Doric colonies in Sicily. Tyrannicism itself created the great mobility of the masses which was detrimental to the quiet development of the colonies.

The presence of the Sicels at the frontiers of the Greek territories was a second specific factor. The gradual Hellenization of this barbaric ethnic element meant a further increase of the population of the χῶρα without immigration from abroad. This same element furnished the tyrants with the mercenary troops which, when they became veterans, expected to be settled within the boundaries of the territory. Thanks to the intrinsic wealth of the island, this grave problem generally found a solution of at least temporary nature, but the presence of the Sicels and the mercenaries had inevitably a permanent influence on the social and political situation in Hellenic Sicily.

The natural wealth of Sicily was another element which contrasted with the conditions of the mother country. Such a fact was for understandable reasons not mentioned by Alcibiades. Fertile plains and valleys produced all the grain and cattle necessary to feed a continually increasing population. Big forests of pine and cypress trees furnished the lumber needed to build commercial and military fleets which kept up the communications overseas and defended the coasts of the island. Sicily's productivity in the agrarian field was legendary as early as the late archaic period. It is enough to record that Gelon, in 480 B.C., offered to the Greek ambassadors, who asked him for help against the Persians, to supply all the Greek military forces with the necessary grain for the entire duration of the war (Herod. VII. 158).

The luxurious life of the Agrigentines was proverbial, and the wealth of the city was famous in the entire Greek world. Empedocles' somewhat ironic remark (*apud* Diog. Laert. VIII. 6.3) is typical: "The Agrigentines live a life so full of delights as if they expected to die tomorrow, but their houses are so well built as if they believed they would live forever."

These two physical factors, the great space and the immense natural wealth of the island, gave to the Greek civilization in Sicily a special tint which was different from that of the mother country. They exercised an important influence on the substance and historical development of Siceliote culture.

Attention should be called to another factor of a different nature, the presence on the island of the ἐπικράτεια of the Carthaginians. The more or less real menace of mighty barbarian and anti-Hellenic forces tended to make the Hellenism of Sicily militant. In spite of the innate differences between the Ionio-Chalcidians and the Dorians, and in spite of the innumerable and bloody conflicts among the πόλεις Ἑλληνίδες of the island, the immediate and permanent presence at the west frontier of an anti-Greek power instilled into the Siceliotes a sense of supreme solidarity and a common pride in their Hellenism, of which we find only rare manifestations in the mother country.

A field in which one can study a specific feature of the Siceliote and the Megalo-Hellenic civilization is the urbanistic one. In the ancient cities of Greece, town planning seems to be almost entirely missing. The old

Fig. 38. City plan of archaic Agrigentum

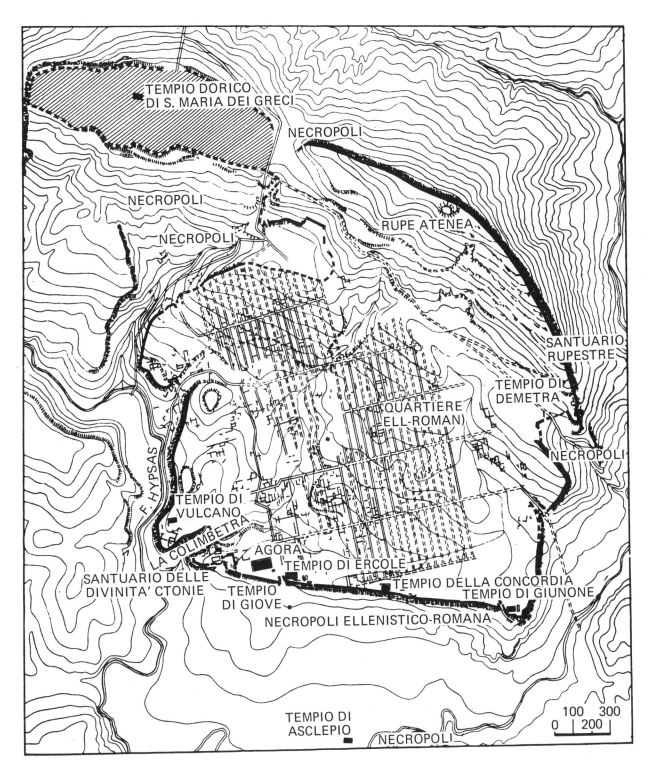

TEMPIO DORICO
DI S. MARIA DEI GRECI

NECROPOLI

NECROPOLI

NECROPOLI

RUPE ATENEA

SANTUARIO
RUPESTRE

TEMPIO DI
DEMETRA

(QUARTIERE
ELL-ROMAN)

NECROPOLI

F. HYPSAS

TEMPIO DI
VULCANO

LA COLIMBETRA

AGORA

TEMPIO DI ERCOLE

TEMPIO DELLA CONCORDIA
TEMPIO DI GIUNONE

SANTUARIO DELLE
DIVINITA' CTONIE

TEMPIO
DI GIOVE

NECROPOLI ELLENISTICO-ROMANA

TEMPIO DI
ASCLEPIO

NECROPOLI

100 | 300

0 | 200

centers like Athens itself grew in an organic way through the centuries from a central nucleus toward the periphery. The result was a confused and disorderly network of streets of the same type as that existing in "vetus Roma," so vividly described by Tacitus (*Ann.* 15.28). Space was limited and old boundary lines between private property were inviolable. To transform a similarly structured city into a regular plan was materially impracticable. Probably the need of it was never even felt.

The situation was fundamentally different when a foundation *ex novo* was concerned, as was the case in a colonial settlement.

The regular town plan and the rectangular street grid were in those cases really the simplest solution. There is no need of an urbanistic genius to "invent" such a system. The new land had to be subdivided in more or less equal lots among the colonists, an easily resolved task as long as there was enough space and the surveyor applied to his operation the straight line and the right angle. Any other solution would have been infinitely more complicated. There came into being in the Greek world, therefore, the urbanistic system which, with questionable right, carries the name of Hippodamus, the famous Ionian architect from Miletus. He rebuilt Piraeus after the Persian wars (Schol. Arist. *Eq.* 327 κατὰ τὰ Μηδικά), and he was probably commissioned with the planning of the colonial city of Thurii in 443 B.C. In his fundamental work, Castagnoli associates him not so much with the principle of the regular street grid as with the refined and developed application of the principle as we meet it during the fifth century B.C.[5]

Thanks to aerophotographic reconnaissance and to the research of Giulio Schmiedt[6] and Dinu Adamesteanu, we are now able to reconstruct with satisfactory certainty the original town plan of the big center of Agrigentum of the sixth century B.C. Its date is thus at least a century earlier than Hippodamus (Fig. 38). The rectangular plan is evident. Six wide thoroughfares (πλατείαι) run in the direction east-west, and a great number of narrower streets (στενοποί) cross them in the direction north-south.

The whole urbanistic layout seems born on the drafting table of a great architect, backed by the absolute power of the founder of the city. One can well imagine the difference between the daily life in a town of this type and that lived in the disorganized labyrinth of the ancient mother cities.

The air photograph of Selinus has revealed a very similar plan, also designed in the archaic age (Fig. 39). The same rationale and the same principle were applied to this city right from its birth.[7]

Long-range town planning in the grand style was applied by the colonists from the very beginning of their enterprises. The planning does not mean that the entire town was built simultaneously. The street grid alone was fixed from the beginning while the individual blocks rose according to the needs of a growing population. Such a development can be documented by archaeological evidence in Morgantina, which received a new rectangular town plan in the period of Timoleon. The Timoleontic edifices are, however, relatively rare, and the ambitious street plan was gradually filled in with buildings during the late fourth and the third centuries B.C.[8]

Once fixed, the street network has a tenacious tendency to remain unchanged through the centuries. Thus, Hellenistic and Roman Agrigentum maintained its archaic plan,[9] and the modern property boundaries in Morgantina are often oriented along the street lines of the fourth century B.C.

The spacious planning of the new cities could not but exert a certain influence on their monumental architecture. Add to these considerations of an aesthetic nature the growing prosperity of the colonies and the spirit of militant Hellenism which inspired the colonists, and the splendid development of the sacred architecture of the Siceliotes becomes far from surprising.

Simple statistics seem rather enlightening. In the entire continental and insular Greece there are recorded sixteen peripteral temples which chronologically cover the sixth and the fifth centuries B.C. Sicily alone has twenty, of which eighteen are archaic. The disproportion is astounding. The city of Selinus counts seven, all archaic, and some of them are of giant size.

The most ancient Selinuntine peripteral temple is also among the biggest. Its total length is approximately seventy-five meters, roughly equal to the Parthenon in Athens. According to Dinsmoor's chronology, it should be dated to about 550 B.C.[10]

Its plan (Fig. 40) shows, first of all, its extraordinary length. The front is hexastyle, but the sides count not fewer than seventeen columns. From a Greek point of view, such proportions are far from orthodox. Also, the

Fig. 39. City plan of archaic Selinus

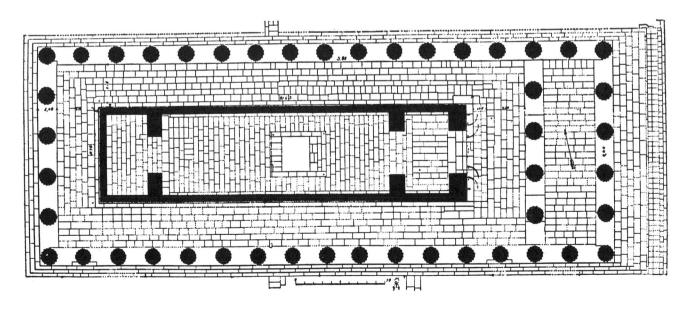

Fig. 40. Plan of Temple C at Selinus

cella is very elongated. It ends in an *adyton* without an *opisthodomus,* a feature rarely met with in Greece proper. The particular accent on the east front should also be observed. In order to obtain such an effect, the architect first of all made a double colonnade on that side, giving to the east end of the building an imposing volumetric impression. Secondly, he built a flight of six steps along the entire east façade, thereby inviting the worshippers to approach the temple in the longitudinal axis of the edifice.

The sculptural decoration (Fig. 41) placed above the inner colonnade of the *pronaos* contributes distinctly to heighten the same desired effect. In the center of the east pediment he placed a polychrome gorgoneion of terracotta, almost three meters high, serving as an impressive focus of attention.

It is true that contemporary comparative material from the mother country is scarce or lacking, but it can, however, be safely said that Temple C of Selinus signifies the beginning of a specific chapter in the history of Siceliote art.

Another monument from Selinus is the metope with Europa on the Bull (Fig. 42). It belonged to an unknown temple dismantled in order to serve for reinforcement of the city wall in 409 B.C. when the Carthaginians laid siege on the city. Stylistically it should be dated to a period slightly more archaic than Temple C. The composition is of particular interest. The big, forceful divine animal breaks the frame of the square metope with its left foreleg and horn. This feature, together with the dolphins under its hoofs, underscores the irresistible march of the animal and its dynamic horizontal movement over the waves. The weight of Europa makes its back curve, but does not break its vigorous advance, giving it, rather, an additional rhythm.

To judge from the material at present in existence, the idea of decorating the metopes of the Doric frieze with sculptural reliefs was a Siceliote "invention." Contemporary temples in the mother country used only painted terracotta plaques for similar decoration.

The ornamental leaf molding along the upper edge of the metope is also worth noticing. Similar things do not occur in Greece proper. To insert such a clearly Ionic

element in an archaic Doric frieze is another sign of the heterodoxy of the Selinuntine artists. It is hardly correct to explain such a phenomenon as only a simple provincialism. Attention should be called to the words of Alcibiades already quoted: "The Siceliotes are a mixed crowd. . . . No one really feels that he has a hometown of his own. . . ."

In the field of art this great mobility of the populations of the Greek coastal cities signified the work of traveling artists, who went wherever the commissions called them. The Ionic and Doric elements in Sicily, which so often were involved in military conflicts and which operated according to such different principles in the field of politics, met harmoniously in the field of art.

There exists a long series of "Ionisms" in the Doric architecture of Sicily, and it is interesting to observe that these tendencies were manifest as early as the first half of the sixth century B.C.[11] They accelerated after the beginning of the fifth century when so many refugees from Ionia migrated to the west to start a new life in the Greek colonies after the Persian conquest of the Greek cities in Asia Minor.

The Siceliote idiosyncrasies during that period are many and well known: to place a double crown of leaves under the echinus of the Doric capital; to add sometimes also an astragalus; to give a clearly Ionic form to the anta capitals (as in Temple GT in Selinus), and many other features unnecessary to enumerate.[12]

It should be remembered that this heterodoxy of the Siceliote architects and stonecarvers is clearly traceable even before the great immigrations of Ionian masters from the east at the beginning of the fifth century. It was a fruit sprung spontaneously from the Siceliote environment, a distinction of their special type of Greek civilization.

So far we have dealt with the Hellenism of the Siceliote colonies, the great and mighty πόλεις Ἑλληνίδες of the coast. Their genuine Hellenism cannot be denied. It is salutary to remember that toward the middle of the eighth century B.C., when the first colonists landed on Sicily's eastern coast, the archaic Greek civilization was still in the very beginning of its development. The colonists came from a still primitive Greece and brought with them a form of civilization answering to these conditions. The development of the Siceliote culture followed in general lines that of the mother country, thanks to the continuous contacts between metropolis and colony. Nonetheless, I believe I have spotted certain elements of Siceliote

Fig. 41. Metope of Temple C at Selinus

culture, characteristic of the island and conditioned by the environment in which lived the colonists of the large and rich island. Such elements gave to Sicilian Hellenism a special and tangible character. It was vigorous and dynamic, and, in a certain sense, also provincial. It did not strive toward classical canons too sophisticated to be understood and accepted by the Siceliotes. They do not seem ever to have meditated over the Delphian device: μηδὲν ἄγαν, "never too much." They shared these features with the colonists of Magna Graecia who also represented a genuine Hellenism, *sui generis*.

Turning to central Sicily and its Hellenized or Greek centers, the situation is for natural reasons a different one. To those centers Hellenism came secondhand, superimposing itself on an indigenous Sicel substratum. Their direct mother cities were not to be found in the distant mother country, but rather in the Siceliote colonies on the coast of the island, which had developed their special form of Greek civilization as early as the sixth century B.C., when the Hellenization of the interior was initiated. The inevitable result was that Greek civilization of central Sicily was a product once removed from the original fountainhead. However, this form of Hellenism too had its genuine aspects.

The excavations at Morgantina have taught us that certain fundamental principles can be traced unchanged even on the small acropolis in the mountains, situated far from the coast. The language was Greek, its social and political system, as far as can be judged from extant architectural remains, was Greek, the art was Greek, although it revealed many features showing its peripheral position in the Hellenic world.

In Morgantina, at least, all this did not exclude the fact that a certain social and economic — and possibly also political — cooperation was conceded to the indigenous Sicels. The Sicels transformed themselves rapidly and on their transformation became conformists. In the fields of art and architecture, no traces of indigenous influence are revealed. In this observation I associate myself fully with what has recently been said by Orlandini in a clarifying paper read at the First International Congress on Sicilian Studies in Palermo, 1965.[13]

In the religious and intellectual fields, as in the artistic one, the current seems to have flowed in one direction only: from the Greeks to the Sicels, not vice versa.

In one single case a reservation seems to be in order. It deals with certain late archaic tombs in Morgantina and Licodia Eubea. The Morgantinian tombs[14] are datable to the decades between 520 and 480 B.C. and are situated on the steep northeast slope of the acropolis. They are chamber tombs cut in the rock. In that sense they follow an age-old Sicel tradition. They were family tombs used for more than a generation, an indigenous tradition. They follow, in that respect, a burial custom alien to real Greeks of this period. All the other evidence brought to light in the excavations confirms that in this period the κτίσμα of Morgantina was profoundly Hellenized, inhabited and governed by Chalcidian Greeks living in peaceful coexistence with the Hellenized Sicels. These very wealthy tombs must have belonged to the governing class, i.e., to the Greek ἔποικοι.

It should be observed that Tomb 4 in this necropolis shows some clearly non-Sicel features. At the far end of the chamber was cut out of the rock a sarcophagus of simple Greek type. Close to the entrance was a rock-cut shaft which had served as a tomb for two bodies. The practice of burying their dead in sarcophagi and shafts is typically Greek, here used in a rock-cut chamber tomb of Sicel type.

The same phenomenon was observed by Orsi in Licodia Eubea.[15] In both cases, the explanation should be the same.

We are confronted with a rare case, to my knowledge, of indigenous influence on the Greek culture of Sicily. Under certain circumstances the Greeks followed the indigenous practice of burying their dead in monumental rock-cut chamber tombs while sticking to their own specific funerary rites of depositing the bodies in sarcophagi or shafts.

It is an interesting phenomenon because the funerary rites of a people generally reflect their ideas of the afterlife, ideas which have a tendency of preserving themselves with a certain tenacity. The mixed rite in Morgantina and Licodia Eubea should, in my opinion, be explained as a gradual development of the relationship between the two ethnic groups through intermarriage. The modifications of the Greek ideas manifest in the

Fig. 42. Europa on the bull. Metope from Selinus

Fig. 43. Terracotta model of a naïskos
from Sabucina

Fig. 44. Terracotta model of a naïskos
from Sabucina, side view

Fig. 45. Terracotta model of a naïskos from Sabucina, detail of acroterium

Fig. 46. Terracotta model of a naïskos from Sabucina, detail of pediment

tomb architecture were, then, a proof of indigenous influence of a kind not difficult to understand, under the given circumstances.

A recent find made in Sabucina near Caltanisetta may serve as an illustration of indigenous reactions to Siceliote art. It deals with an ex-voto dedicated by a Sicel artisan in a small Greek temple. It was found in a dump of votive material outside the walls of the city. It is a small terracotta model of the naïskos where the object itself was once offered. Orlandini has already published it with his usual promptness and clarity.[16]

It is a portable model (Figs. 43–44), possibly used in sacred processions, of a small distyle-prostyle temple, executed with much care and childish wealth of detail. Seen from the side, it reveals the construction of the roof with its pantiles, cover tiles and its big *kalypteres hegemones*. In that sense, it constitutes a precious document for the reconstruction of these Greek naïskoi which now survive only in their rough stone foundations and their fragmentary fictile decoration.

Of special interest to us is the way in which the Greek decoration is rendered by the hands of the Sicel ceramist. The equestrian acroterion which crowns the front pediment renders a Geloan prototype in an inorganic and stylized manner (Fig. 45). The artisan strove toward expressing the figure in an additive manner. The harness and the bridle of the horse interested him in the same degree as did the totality of the figure. The little rider is poorly understood, and the unity of the composition, as well as its dynamism, escaped him. *Mutatis mutandis,* the same observations can be made with regard to the heads which adorn the pediment (Fig. 46). Their position re-

minds one of the antefixes on the Etruscan temple model from Nemi.[17] They seem to have been applied to the *mutuli* of the roof. Orlandini has rightly interpreted them as a Silenus head and a gorgoneion. While the latter is recognizable by the tongue which hangs out of the open mouth, the primitive coroplast was unable to express the less characteristic features of the Silenus.

A comparison between the miniature product of the local ceramist and a true gorgoneion from Morgantina (Fig. 21) reveals immediately the incapability of the artisan to understand and render in convincing form the vigorous character of the original. Instead of the terrible apotropaic form of the mythological monster, he produced a sterile iconographic formula which the Greeks themselves probably had difficulty in understanding.

This single example may suffice to indicate the limitations of the Sicels to absorb Greek archaic forms on the one side, and on the other the absolute independence of the Greeks from indigenous arts and crafts.

This principle is valid for the archaic period of the sixth century B.C. which represents the first and disconcerting contact between the two ethnic elements. As time passed, the assimilation between the Greeks and the indigenous population became almost complete. Then, it was no longer necessary to be a Greek by birth to become a good coroplast.

It is obvious that the assimilation process signified the absorbing of the indigenous element by the Greeks, rather than vice versa.

When that process had come to an end, after three or four generations, the Hellenization of central Sicily was completed.

CHAPTER 1

Notes

1. T. J. Dunbabin, "Minos and Daidalos in Sicily," *BSR*, XVI(= n.s. III) (1948), 1–18. Cf. also idem, *The Western Greeks* (Oxford: Clarendon Press, 1948), pp. 41, 318, 341, 353–54, 413–14.

2. J. Bérard, *La colonisation grecque de l'Italie méridionale et de la Sicile dans l'antiquité*, 2d ed. (Paris: Presses Universitaires de France, 1957), pp. 417–33.

3. G. Pugliese Carratelli, "Minos e Cocalos," *Kokalos,* II (1956), 89–103.

4. G. Becatti, "La leggenda di Dedalo," *Röm. Mitt.*, LX–LXI (1953–54), 22–36.

5. E. Manni, "Minosse ed Eracle nella Sicilia dell' età del bronzo," *Kokalos*, VIII (1962), 6–29.

6. Ibid., p. 20.

7. W. Taylour, *Mycenaean Pottery in Italy and Adjacent Areas* (Cambridge: At the University Press, 1958).

8. Ibid., pp. 16–17, nos. 2–5.

9. E. De Miro, "Heraclea Minoa," *NSc.*, ser. 8, XII (1958), 232–87, and idem, *Eraclea Minoa* (breve guida), (Agrigento: Soprintendenza alle Antichità, 1958), with additional bibliography.

10. Heracleides Ponticus, in *FHG*, II (Paris, 1848), pp. 220–21, fragm. 29.

11. P. Griffo, "Sull' identificazione di Camico con l'odierna S. Angelo Muxaro a nord-ovest di Agrigento," *Arch. Stor. Sic. Orient.*, ser. 4, VII (1954), fasc. I–III, pp. 58–78. J. Bérard, op. cit., p. 423. E. Manni is of another opinion, which he expresses in his valuable book *Sicilia pagana* (Palermo: S. F. Flaccovio, 1963), pp. 54–57. I prefer Manni's opinion.

12. G. Becatti, *Oreficerie antiche dalle minoiche alle barbariche* (Roma: Istituto Poligrafico dello Stato, 1955), pp. 183–84, nos. 302 a, b, 303 a, b.

13. A. Evans, *The Palace of Minos at Knossos* (London: Macmillan and Co.), vol. IV, pt. II (1935), 959–1018; plan: ibid., p. 1001, fig. 952.

14. G. Becatti, "La leggenda di Dedalo," *Röm. Mitt.*, LX–LXI (1953–54), 31–32, and note 34. – A. Evans, *The Palace of Minos at Knossos*, vol. II, pt. II (1928), 391–96; plan: fig. 224 (for the House of the Chancel Screen), and pp. 396–413, plans: figs. 227, 228 (for the "Royal Villa").

15. P. Orsi, "Necropoli sicula presso Siracusa con vasi e bronzi micenei," *Mon. Ant.*, vol. II (1893), cols. 5–36 (for Cozzo del Pantano). Idem, "Thapsos," *Mon. Ant.*, vol. VI (1895), cols. 89–150 (for Thapsos).

16. P. Orsi, "Thapsos," *Mon. Ant.*, vol. VI (1895), col. 137.

17. E. A. Freeman, *The History of Sicily from the Earliest Times* (Oxford: Clarendon Press), vol. I (1891), 113 and 502.

18. E. Pais, *Storia della Sicilia e della Magna Grecia* (Torino, Palermo: Clausen, 1894), pp. 231 ff.

19. L. Pareti, *Sicilia antica* (Palermo: Palumbo, 1959), pp. 26–27. Idem, "Studi siciliani ed italiote," *Contributi alla scienza dell'antichità*, I (1920), 262–71.

20. *RE*, vol. XV (1932), cols. 1855–57.

21. *BPI*, XXIII (1897), pp. 12–13 and pl. 2, figs. 8–9 (for the bronze basins); ibid., pp. 10–12 and pl. 2, figs. 1–2 (for the knife blades). L. Bernabò Brea, *Sicily before the Greeks* (London: Thames and Hudson, 1957), pp. 131–32 and fig. 26.

22. For Mycenaean pottery from these places see W. Taylour, op. cit., pp. 56–60 and pl. 9, figs. 1–3, 12 (Thapsos); pp. 62–63 and pl. 9, figs. 6–7 (Matrensa); p. 61 (Floridia); pp. 61–62 and pl. 9, fig. 11 (Cozzo del Pantano); and pp. 60–61 (Molinello).

23. E. Sjöqvist, "Heracles in Sicily," *Opusc. Rom.*, IV (1962), 117–23.

24. M. P. Nilsson, *The Mycenaean Origin of Greek Mythology* (New York: The Norton Library, 1963), chap. III, pp. 187–220.

25. E. Sjöqvist, op. cit., pp. 120–21.

26. W. Taylour, op. cit., p. 64.

27. E. Sjöqvist, "Excavations at Morgantina (Serra Orlando) 1959. Preliminary Report IV," *AJA*, 64 (1960), p. 134 and pl. 30, fig. 39 a–b.

Chapter 2

1. P. Orsi, "La necropoli sicula del Plemmirio (Siracusa)," *BPI*, XVII (1891), 115–39. The sword here referred to is discussed on pp. 121–23, and illustrated on pl. XI, fig. 10. Cf. W. Taylour, op. cit., p. 188.

2. L. Bernabò Brea, op. cit., pp. 131–32 and fig. 26. *BPI*, XXIII (1897), pp. 12–13 and pl. 2, figs. 8–9.

3. W. Taylour, op. cit., p. 70, with bibliographical informations. Cf. also L. Bernabò Brea, op. cit., pp. 126–27 and fig. 24, pp. 134–35 and pl. 55.

4. R. Carpenter, "Phoenicians in the West," *AJA*, 62 (1958), 35–53, considers the Thucydidean information based on the Greek historian's false assumption, that Homer's mentioning of the Phoenicians in the *Odyssey* (cf. below note 7) reflected actual historical events after the Trojan war. This may very well be the case. Lack of archaeological and collateral evidence for the permanently established presence of Phoenicians in the West before the historical Greek colonization makes Carpenter discard Thucydides' statement as groundless.

5. A classical and fundamental work is that by P. Bosch-Gimpera, "Fragen der Chronologie der phönizischen Kolonisation in Spanien," *Klio*, XXII (1928), 345–68. He reaches the tentative and well-balanced conclusions that Tartessus and its neighboring place Gades (Cadiz) on the Atlantic coast of Spain close to the inexhaustible silver mines of Sierra Morena were not permanent installations nor capitals of a colonial province, but trading emporia and market places where Phoenicians appeared at an early period. The temporary character of these installations may — as in Sicily — account for the lack of material archaeological evidence for their existence. G. Garbini, "I Fenici in Occidente," *Studi Etr.*, XXXIV (1966), 111–47, summarizes the discussion up to date, adds a very useful bibliography, and contributes many interesting and original ideas. Cf. V. Tusa, "La questione fenicio-punica in Sicilia," *Studi Annibalici: Atti del convegno svoltosi a Cortona-Tuoro sul Trasimeno-Perugia ottobre 1961* (Cortona: Tipografia Commerciale, 1964), pp. 37–55. See also: S. Moscati, "La questione fenicia," *Rend. Acc. Linc.*, ser. VIII, vol. XVIII (1963), 483–506. Idem, *The World of the Phoenicians* (London: Weidenfeld and Nicolson, 1968) with bibliography. I. Schifman, "Die phönikische Kolonisation des westlichen Mittelmeeres," *Das Altertum*, X (1964), 195–201.

   The negative attitude of J. Beloch, "Die Phoeniker am aegaeischen Meer," *Rhein. Mus.*, Neue Folge, XLIX (1894), 111–32, upheld and reinforced with more recent arguments by R. Carpenter, op. cit. (above, note 4), must still be respected, but has not gained in strength.

6. W. F. Albright, "New Light on the Early History of the Phoenician Colonization," *BASOR*, LXXXIII (1941), 14–22.

7. S. Chiappisi, *Il Melqart di Sciacca e la questione fenicia in Sicilia* (Roma: G. Bardi, 1961). V. Tusa, op. cit., (above, note 5), considers the statuette to prove the Phoenician presence in Sicily in the eleventh century B.C., to which time the statuette should be dated. To me it seems only to prove that it fell overboard from a Phoenician merchant's ship off the coast of Sicily at that time. Nothing can be known of where the cargo was destined. It tells us, of course, nothing of permanent Phoenician installations in Sicily at that time.

   Later Punic material found in Sicily is usefully gathered and illustrated by Tusa in the same article.

8. B. H. Warmington, *Carthage* (London: Robert Hale Limited, 1960), p. 20. D. Harden, *The Phoenicians* (London: Thames and Hudson, 1962), p. 66.

9. *SCE*, IV, pt. II (1948), pp. 440 note 2, 497, 506. G. F. Hill, *Catalogue of the Greek Coins of Cyprus* (London: British Museum, 1904), pp. xl–xli and 21–23.

10. *SCE*, IV, pt. II (1948), 437–39.

11. P. Cintas, "Deux campagnes de fouille à Utique," *Karthago*, II (1951), 1–88. Idem, "Nouvelles recherches à Utique," *Karthago*, V (1954), 89–154. Cf. R. Carpenter, "A Note on the Foundation Date of Carthage," *AJA*, 68 (1964), 178.

12. E. Forrer, "Karthago wurde erst 673–663 v. Chr. gegründet," *Festschrift Franz Dornseiff zum 65. Geburtstag*, herausgegeben von H. Kusch (Leipzig: VEB Bibliographisches Institut, 1953), pp. 85–93.

13. E. Frézouls, "Une nouvelle hypothèse sur la fondation de Carthage," *BCH*, LXXIX (1955), 153–76. It should be noted that Å. Åkerström, "Der geometrische Stil in Italien," *Acta Inst. Rom. Suec.*, IX (1943), 162–64, also inclines toward a low date of the foundation of Carthage.

14. For the difference in attitude toward the Phoenicians between the *Iliad* and the *Odyssey* see R. Carpenter, "Phoenicians in the West," *AJA*, 62 (1958), 35–36.

15. On the foundation dates of Megara Hyblaea and Syracuse see G. Vallet and F. Villard, "Les dates de fondation de Megara Hyblaea et de Syracuse," *BCH*, LXXVI (1952), 289–346.

16. For a stringent and logical discussion of the historical sources bearing on the chronology of the Greek colonies I refer to M. T. Piraino, "Sulla cronologia delle fondazioni siceliote," *Kokalos*, III (1957), 123–28, with full bibliography. Mrs. Piraino champions on good grounds the higher chronology. On the higher chronology of Naxos and Megara see also A. Schenk von Stauffenberg, *Trinakria* (München: R. Oldenburg Verlag, 1963), pp. 351–54 with his useful summary of arguments.

17. G. Vallet and F. Villard, op. cit., pp. 335–45. Cf. also M. T. Piraino, op. cit., p. 126 and note 13. Also G. Vallet, "Rhégion et Zancle: histoire, commerce et civilisation des cités chalcidiennes du détroit de Messine," *BEFAR*, CLXXXIX (1958), 55–58, where the archaeological material and the literary sources are jointly considered.

18. P. Pelagatti, "Naxos – relazione preliminare delle campagne di scavo 1961–64," *Bd'A*, 1964, pp. 149–65 and figs. 40–43.

19. A. Brelich, "La religione greca in Sicilia," *Kokalos*, X–XI (1964–65), *Atti del I congresso internazionale di studi sulla Sicilia antica*, pp. 35–54, argues (especially pp. 45–46) that Apollo Archegetes of the colonists was not the Delphian, but the Delian Apollo. Such a hypothesis is hard to reconcile with the well-documented contacts between Delphi and colonies from earliest times, summarized by M. P. Nilsson, *Geschichte der griechischen Religion*, I (Dritte, durchgesehene und ergänzte Auflage; München: C. H. Beck'sche Verlagsbuchhandlung, 1967), pp. 637–40. Brelich's arguments for the Delian Apollo are based on his presumed historical precedence, on the relatively late rise of Delphi as a pan-Hellenic center, and on the pan-Ionian character of the Delian cult. None of these arguments seem strong enough to corroborate his ingenious hypothesis.

20. Cf. Plato, *Laws*, V. 738 B ff., whence Cicero obviously lifted his phrase.

Chapter 3

1. G. Rizza, "Siculi e greci sui colli di Leontini," *Cronache di archeologia e di storia dell'arte*, I (1962), pp. 3–27 and pls. I–IV. Cf. also L. Bernabò Brea, op. cit., pp. 172–73, fig. 40, and pls. 67–68.

2. P. Orsi, "Le necropoli di Licodia Eubea ed i vasi geometrici del quarto periodo siculo," *Röm. Mitt.*, XIII (1898), 305–66.

3. Idem, "Sepolcri di transizione dalla civiltà sicula alla greca," *Röm. Mitt.*, XXIV (1909), 59–73 (pt. I. Ipogeo siculo grecizante di Licodia Eubea).

4. G. Vallet, "La colonisation chalcidienne et l'hellénisation de la Sicile orientale," *Kokalos*, VIII (1962), 35.

5. P. Orsi, "Le necropoli di Licodia Eubea ed i vasi geometrici del quarto periodo siculo," *Röm. Mitt.*, XIII (1898), 327–28. G. Vallet, "La colonisation chalcidienne et l'hellénisation de la Sicile orientale," *Kokalos*, VIII (1962), 34–35.

6. P. Orsi, "Le necropoli di Licodia Eubea ed i vasi geometrici del quarto periodo siculo," *Röm. Mitt.*, XIII (1898), 327.

7. P. Orsi, "D'una città greca a Terravecchia presso Grammichele in provincia di Catania," *Mon. Ant.*, vol. VII (1897), cols. 201–74. Idem, "Necropoli e stazioni sicule di transizione. V. Necropoli al Molinello della Badia presso Grammichele," *BPI*, XXXI (1905), 96–133. Idem, "Anathemata di una città siculo-greca a Terravecchia di Grammichele (Catania)," *Mon. Ant.*, vol. XVIII (1908), cols. 121–68. Cf. also L. Bernabò Brea, E. Militello and S. La Piana, "Mineo (Catania). La necropoli detta Molino della Badia: nuove tombe in contrada Madonna del Piano," *NSc.*, 1969, pp. 210–75.

8. Cf. G. Vallet, "La colonisation chalcidienne et l'hellénisation de la Sicile orientale," *Kokalos*, VIII (1962), 36–37.

9. P. Orsi, "Fittili con un verso del comico Frinico e varie scoperte," *NSc.*, 1920, pp. 336–37.

10. G. M. A. Richter, *Kouroi: Archaic Greek Youths* (London: The Phaidon Press, 1960), p. 146, no. 185, and figs. 544–46.

11. P. Orsi, "Anathemata di una città siculo-greca a Terravecchia di Grammichele (Catania)," *Mon. Ant.*, Vol. XVIII (1908), col. 167. Cf. B. Pace, *Arte e civiltà della Sicilia antica*, 4 vols. (Milano: Società anonima editrice Dante Alighieri [Albrighi, Segati & C.], 1935–49), I. p. 202 and note 3.

12. Cf. also the principle of Chalcidian liberalism expressed by G. Vallet, "La colonisation chalcidienne et l'hellénisation de la Sicile orientale," *Kokalos*, VIII (1962), especially pp. 48–51.

13. See my reports from the excavations at Morgantina on the Lower Acropolis in *AJA*, 64 (1960), pp. 134–35, and pl. 30 ("Preliminary Report IV"); *AJA*, 66 (1962), pp. 141–42, and pl. 34 ("Preliminary Report VI"); *AJA*, 68 (1964), pp. 145–46, and pl. 41, fig. 21, pl. 46, figs. 18–22 ("Preliminary Report VIII"). Cf. also my article "I greci a Morgantina," *Kokalos*, VIII (1962), pp. 58–60, and pls. 3–4.

14. On the ashlar wall, see my above-mentioned reports in *AJA*, 64 (1960), pp. 134–35, and pl. 30, figs. 40–41; *AJA*, 66 (1962), 141.

15. Further evidence for a Greek settlement came in an inscribed shard with the letters ꓭ Ε on a matte-glazed hydria or amphora neck and it is tempting to connect this graffito (restored Θεῶ) with a number of pan and cover tiles found in the same context.

16. E. Sjöqvist, "Excavations at Serra Orlando (Morgantina). Preliminary Report II," *AJA*, 62 (1958), p. 158 and pl. 29, figs. 10–11. Idem, "Excavations at Morgantina (Serra Orlando) 1961. Preliminary Report VI," *AJA*, 66 (1962), 143.

17. Idem, "Excavations at Serra Orlando (Morgantina). Preliminary Report II," *AJA*, 62 (1958), p. 158, and pl. 29, fig. 11; pl. 30, figs. 12–15; pl. 31, fig. 16 a–d.

18. Idem, "Excavations at Morgantina (Serra Orlando) 1961. Preliminary Report VI," *AJA*, 66 (1962), p. 143, and pl. 35, figs. 33–34; pl. 36, fig. 35.

Chapter 4

1. See the above-mentioned article by G. Vallet, "La colonisation chalcidienne et l'hellénisation de la Sicile orientale," *Kokalos*, VIII (1962), 30–51.

2. A. Di Vita, "La penetrazione siracusana nella Sicilia sud-orientale alla luce delle più recenti scoperte archeologiche," *Kokalos*, II (1956), 177–205.

3. For the excavations at Helorus during the years 1899, 1927, 1958–59, and 1961 see P. Orsi et al., "Eloro," *Mon. Ant.*, vol. XLVII (1966), cols. 203–340 with earlier bibliography.

4. L. Bernabò Brea, *Akrai* (Catania, 1956), pp. 21–25.

5. Di Vita, op. cit., pp. 186–96.

6. Di Vita, op. cit., p. 193.

7. Di Vita, op. cit., p. 185.

8. Di Vita, op. cit., pp. 196–98.

9. P. Orsi, "Ragusa (Ὕβλα Ἡραία). Di alcuni sepolcri spettanti all'arcaica necropoli e di altre minori scoperte," *NSc.*, 1892, pp. 321–32. Idem, "Ragusa. Nuove esplorazioni nella necropoli di Hybla Heraia," *NSc.*, 1899, pp. 402–18.

10. A. Di Vita, "Recenti scoperte archeologiche in provincia di Ragusa," *Arch. St. Sir.*, II (1956), pp. 41–44, and pl. 2.

11. A. M. Fallico, "Ragusa. Esplorazione di necropoli tarde," *NSc.*, 1967, pp. 407–18.

12. A. Di Vita, "La penetrazione siracusana nella Sicilia sud-orientale alla luce delle più recenti scoperte archeologiche," *Kokalos*, II (1956), 198–99.

13. Philistus, in *FHG*, vol. I, p. 186, fragm. 8. Cf. Thucy. VI. 5.3.

14. D. Adamesteanu, "Butera: Piano della Fiera, Consi e Fontana Calda," *Mon. Ant.*, vol. XLIV (1958), cols. 205–672.

15. D. Adamesteanu, "Nouvelles fouilles à Gela et dans l'arrière-pays," *Rev. Arch.*, XLIX (1957), 158.

16. On Monte Bubbonia, see D. Adamesteanu, "Ἀνάκτορα o sacelli," *Archeol. Class.*, VII (1955), pp. 179–82, and pls. LXXIV–LXXV.

17. Ibid., pp. 183–86, and pls. LXXV–LXXVII.

18. For Monte Bubbonia: P. Orsi, "Monte Bubbonia (Comune di Mazzarino). Città e necropoli sicula dei tempi greci," *NSc.*, 1905, pp. 447–49. Idem, "M. Bubbonia (Commune di Mazzarino)," *NSc.*, 1907, pp. 497–98. For Monte San Mauro: P. Orsi, "Di una anonima città siculo-greca a Monte S. Mauro presso Caltagirone (scavi dal 1903 al 1905)," *Mon. Ant.*, vol. XX (1911), cols. 729–850.

19. See the above-cited article by D. Adamesteanu, "Ἀνάκτορα o sacelli," *Archeol. Class.*, VII (1955), pp. 179–86, and pls. LXXIV–LXXVII. Cf. also idem, "Nouvelles fouilles à Géla et dans l'arrière-pays," *Rev. Arch.*, XLIX (1957), 165–70.

20. P. Orsi, "Di una anonima città siculo-greca a Monte S. Mauro presso Caltagirone (scavi dal 1903 al 1905)," *Mon. Ant.*, vol. XX (1911), pl. V.

21. L. Bernabò Brea, "L'Athenaion di Gela e le sue terrecotte architettoniche," *Annuario Scuola Atene*, XXVII–XXIX (Nuova Serie XI–XIII) (1949–51), pls. II–III.

22. D. Adamesteanu, "Nouvelles fouilles à Géla et dans l'arrière-pays," *Rev. Arch.*, XLIX (1957), 147–70. Idem, "Scavi e scoperte nella provincia di Caltanissetta dal 1951 al 1957," *NSc.*, 1958, pp. 335–50 (Monte Desusino); 350–62 (Milingiana); 383–87 (Lavanca Nero). Idem, "Note di topografia siceliota. Parte I," *Kokalos*, IX (1963), pp. 26–31 (Monte Desusino); 32–35 (Lavanca Nero).

23. E. De Miro, "La fondazione di Agrigento e l'ellenizzazione del territorio fra il Salso e il Platani," *Kokalos*, VIII (1962), 122–52. Cf. D. Adamesteanu, "Rapporti tra greci e indigeni alla luce delle nuove scoperte in Sicilia," *Atti del settimo congresso internazionale di archeologia classica*, 3 vols. (Roma: "L'Erma" di Bretschneider, 1961), Vol. II, pp. 45–52.

24. E. A. Freeman, *The History of Sicily from the Earliest Times*, 4 vols. (Oxford: Clarendon Press, 1891–94), Vol. II, pp. 69–70.

25. For some results of this topographical research concerning the old road system in the eastern and southern parts of Sicily, see for instance D. Adamesteanu, "L'ellenizzazione della Sicilia ed il momento di Ducezio," *Kokalos*, VIII (1962), pp. 167–98, and pls. LXXX–XCIII. Idem, "Note su alcune vie siceliote di penetrazione," *Kokalos*, VIII (1962), pp. 199–209, and pls. XCIV–XCIX. Idem, "Note di topografia siceliota. Parte I," *Kokalos*, IX (1963), pp. 19–48, and pls. I–XVIII.

26. Area V, especially trench 3. See my reports: "Excavations at Morgantina (Serra Orlando) 1961. Preliminary Report VI," *AJA*, 66 (1962), pp. 142–43, and pl. 35, figs. 30–31; "Excavations at Morgantina (Serra Orlando) 1963. Preliminary Report VIII," *AJA*, 68 (1964), 144–45; and the report by R. Stillwell, "Excavations at Morgantina (Serra Orlando) 1962. Preliminary Report VII," *AJA*, 67 (1963), 170. Cf. also my article "I greci a Morgantina," *Kokalos*, VIII (1962), pp. 56–58, and pl. 2.

CHAPTER 5

1. Cf. also A. Schenk von Stauffenberg, "Dorieus," *Historia*, IX (1960), 190–98.

2. D. Adamesteanu, "L'ellenizzazione della Sicilia ed il momento di Ducezio," *Kokalos*, VIII (1962), 167–98.

3. D. Adamesteanu, op. cit., pp. 169–74.

4. See D. Adamesteanu, op. cit., pp. 167–98.

5. D. Adamesteanu, "Nouvelles fouilles à Géla et dans l'arrière-pays," *Rev. Arch.*, XLIX (1957), 174–75. Idem, "L'ellenizzazione della Sicilia ed il momento di Ducezio," *Kokalos*, VIII (1962), 185–86.

6. D. Adamesteanu, "L'ellenizzazione della Sicilia ed il momento di Ducezio," *Kokalos*, VIII (1962), 195–96.

7. P. Orlandini, "Sabucina. A) Scoperte varie. B) Prima campagna di scavo (1962). Rapporto preliminare," *Archeol. Class.*, XV (1963), pp. 86–96, and pls. XX–XI. Idem, "Sabucina. La seconda campagna di scavo (1964). Rapporto preliminare," *Archeol. Class.*, XVII (1965), pp. 133–40, and pls. XLVII–LXIII. Idem, "Sabucina: la terza campagna di scavo (1966). Rapporto preliminare," *Archeol. Class.*, XX (1968), pp. 151–56, and pls. LVII–LXV.

8. P. Orlandini, "Sabucina: la terza campagna di scavo (1966). Rapporto preliminare," *Archeol. Class.*, XX (1968), 151–56.

9. D. Adamesteanu, "Nouvelles fouilles à Géla et dans l'arrière-pays," *Rev. Arch.*, XLIX (1957), 174–75. Cf. also De Miro, "La fondazione di Agrigento e l'ellenizzazione del territorio fra il Salso e il Platani," *Kokalos*, VIII (1962), 143–44; and P. Orlandini, "L'espansione di Gela nella Sicilia centro-meridionale," *Kokalos*, VIII (1962), 94.

10. D. Adamesteanu, "Gibil-Gabib (Caltanissetta), Scavi e ricerche archeologiche," *NSc.*, 1958, pp. 407–8. Cf. also P. Orlandini, "L'ellenizzazione di Gela nella Sicilia centro-meridionale," *Kokalos*, VIII (1962), 99–100.

11. On the policy in Carthage of acquiring a territorial empire in Africa see B. H. Warmington, *Carthage* (London: Robert Hale Ltd, 1960), pp. 51–53 and 73–74.

12. Warmington, op. cit., p. 74.

13. *IG*.I².:19. Cf. A. E. Raubitschek, "Greek Inscriptions," *Hesp.*, XII (1943), p. 18, note 29. Cf. also H. Wentker, *Sizilien und Athen* (Heidelberg: Quelle & Meyer, 1956), pp. 49, 65, and 168–69; Anmerkungen 301–4.

14. See also H. Wentker, op. cit.

15. D. Adamesteanu, "Nouvelles fouilles à Géla et dans l'arrière-pays," *Rev. Arch.*, XLIX (1957), 173. P. Orlandini, "L'espansione di Gela nella Sicilia centro-meridionale," *Kokalos*, VIII (1962), pp. 100–106, and pls. XVIII–XXVIII. Idem, "Sabucina. A) Scoperte varie. B) Prima campagna di scavo (1962). Rapporto preliminare," *Archeol. Class.*, XV (1963), pp. 86–96, and pls. XX–XL. Idem, "Sabucina. La seconda campagna di scavo (1964). Rapporto preliminare," *Archeol. Class.*, XVII (1965), pp. 133–40, and pls. XLVII–LXIII. Idem. "Sabucina: la terza campagna di scavo (1966). Rapporto preliminare," *Archeol. Class.*, XX (1968), pp. 151–56, and pls. LVII–LXV.

16. D. Adamesteanu, "Nouvelles fouilles à Géla et dans l'arrière-pays," *Rev. Arch.*, XLIX (1957), 174–75. Idem,

"Monte Saraceno ed il problema della penetrazione rodio-cretese nella Sicilia meridionale," *Archeol. Class.*, VIII (1956), 138–39. Idem, "L'opera di Timoleonte nella Sicilia centro-meridionale vista attraverso gli scavi e le ricerche archeologiche," *Kokalos*, IV (1958), 50–52. Idem, "L'ellenizzazione dell Sicilia ed il momento di Ducezio," *Kokalos*, VIII (1962), 185–86. P. Orlandini, "Arule arcaiche a rilievo nel Museo Nazionale di Gela," *Röm. Mitt.*, LXVI (1959), 100. Cf. also *AJA*, 61 (1957), 385, and *AJA*, 66 (1962), 400–401. E. De Miro, "La fondazione di Agrigento e l'ellenizzazione del territorio fra il Salso e il Platani," *Kokalos*, VIII (1962), pp. 143–44, and pls. LV–LX.

17. D. Adamesteanu, "Le fortificazione ad aggere nella Sicilia centro-meridionale," *Rend. Acc. Linc.*, ser. VIII, vol. XI (1956), pp. 367–68. Idem, "Gibil-Gabib (Caltanissetta). Scavi e richerche archeologiche," *NSc.*, 1958, pp. 387–408 (with earlier bibliography). Idem, "L'opera di Timoleonte nella Sicilia centro-meridionale vista attraverso gli scavi e le ricerche archeologiche," *Kokalos*, IV (1958), 52–54. Cf. also P. Orlandini, "L'espansione di Gela nella Sicilia centro-meridionale," *Kokalos*, VIII (1962), pp. 99–100, and pls. XV–XVIII.

18. P. Orlandini, "L'espansione di Gela nella Sicilia centro-meridionale," *Kokalos*, VIII (1962), p. 107, and pls. XXIX–XXXI. Cf. also, for this and the other places, the bibliography on archeological excavations in Gela Provincia di Caltanissetta given in *NSc.*, 1960, pp. 68–69.

19. Cf. P. Orlandini, "L'espansione di Gela nella Sicilia centro-meridionale," *Kokalos*, VIII (1962), 106.

20. Cf. the articles in the above-mentioned volume IV of the review *Kokalos* (1958).

CHAPTER 6

1. This chapter has also been published in a revised Italian version: "La grecità della Sicilia antica," in *Opusc. Rom.*, VI (= *Acta Inst. Rom. Suec.*, XXIX) (1968), 129–43.

2. Cf. also S. Säflund, "Jonisches und Dorisches in Magna Graecia," *Opuscula Archaeologica*, II (= *Acta Inst. Rom. Suec.*, V) (1941), 77–89.

3. For the historic evaluation of Pindar's Sicilian odes, see A. Schenk von Stauffenberg, *Trinakria. Sizilien und Grossgriechenland in archaischer und frühklassischer Zeit* (München & Wien: R. Oldenburg Verlag, 1963), pp. 221–73.

4. Q. Cataudella, "Tragedie di Eschilo nella Siracusa di Gerone," *Kokalos*, X–XI (1964–65), 371–98.

5. F. Castagnoli, *Ippodamo di Mileto e l'urbanistica a pianta ortogonale* (Roma: De Luca Editore, 1956), p. 65. Cf. also idem, "Recenti ricerche sull'urbanistica ippodamea," *Archeol. Class.*, XV (1963), 180–97 (with bibliographical notes).

6. G. Schmiedt and P. Griffo, *Agrigento antica dalle fotografie aeree e dai recenti scavi* ([Estratto da l'Universo]; Firenze: Istituto Geografico Militare, 1958). G. Schmiedt, "Applicazioni della fotografia aerea in ricerche estensive di topografia antica in Sicilia," *Kokalos*, III (1957), pp. 20–22, and pls. 1–4.

7. A. Giuliano, *Urbanistica delle città greche* (Milano: Il Saggiatore, 1966), pp. 50–54. Here I should like to add the following remark, that the rectangular and regular town plan seems to be a solution which appears spontaneously in the Greek colonies, wherever they were founded. There are examples of the same principle used also in Ionian colonial territory, as in the case of Old Smyrna (J. M. Cook, "Old Smyrna," *BSA*, LIII–LIV [1958–59], 2–34). Cf. idem, *The Greeks in Ionia and the East* (London: Thames and Hudson, 1962), pp. 68 ff.

A similar solution seems natural also in non-Greek regions in the Orient, as C. Nylander has recently demonstrated. C. Nylander, "Remarks on the Urartian Acropolis at Zernaki Tepe," *Orientalia Suecana*, XIV–XV (1964–65), 141–54. This city was a fortress, founded for defense against Assyrians and Cimmerians, and as such it was a foundation "ex novo" in the seventh century B.C. Zernaki Tepe, with its probable Mesopotamian derivation and inspiration, demonstrates that the regular and rectangular town plan was not exclusively Greek, but had an almost universal valuation in archaic times in the Mediterranean region and the Near East, in the construction of new cities for special purposes, whether colonial or military.

8. E. Sjöqvist, "Timoleonte e Morgantina," *Kokalos*, IV (1958), 107–18. R. Stillwell, "Excavations at Morgantina (Serra Orlando) 1960. Preliminary Report V," *AJA*, 65 (1961), p. 279, and pl. 92, fig. 5.

9. E. De Miro, "Il quartiere ellenistico-romano di Agrigento," *Rend. Acc. Linc.*, serie VII, vol. XII (1957), 137–38.

10. W. B. Dinsmoor, *The Architecture of Ancient Greece*, 3d ed., rev. and enl. (London: B. T. Batsford Ltd., 1950), p. 83.

11. G. Säflund, op. cit.

12. For complete information I refer to the fundamental work by L. T. Shoe (Mrs. B. D. Merrit), *Profiles of Western Greek Mouldings* (= *Papers and Monographs of the American Academy in Rome*, XIV [1952]), pp. 9–20.

13. P. Orlandini, "Arte indigena e colonizzazione greca in Sicilia," *Kokalos*, X–XI (1964–65), 539–44.

14. E. Sjöqvist, "Excavations at Serra Orlando (Morgantina). Preliminary Report II," *AJA*, 62 (1958), p. 158, and pl. 29, figs. 10–11; pl. 30, figs. 12–15; pl. 31, figs. 16 a–d. Idem, "Excavations at Morgantina (Serra Orlando) 1961. Preliminary Report VI," *AJA*, 66 (1962), p. 143, and pl. 35, figs. 33–34; pl. 36, fig. 35.

15. P. Orsi, "Sepolcri di transizione della civiltà sicula alla greca. I. Ipogeo siculo grecizzante di Licodia Euba,' *Röm. Mitt.*, XXIV (1909), pp. 61–62, and fig. 1.

16. P. Orlandini, "Sabucina. A) Scoperte varie. B) Prima campagna di scavo (1962). Rapporto preliminare," *Archeol. Class.*, XV (1963), p. 88, and pls. XXVII–XXVIII. Idem, "L'espansione di Gela nella Sicilia centro-meridionale," *Kokalos*, VIII (1962), pp. 103–6, and pls. XXVII–XXVIII.

17. A. Andrén, "Architectural Terracottas from Etrusco-Italic Temples: Text," *Acta Inst. Rom. Suec.*, VI (1940), pp. XXXI–XXXII, and figs. 5–6.

Bibliography

ADAMESTEANU, DINU. "Ἀνάκτορα o sacelli," *Archeol. Class.*, VII (1955), 179–86.

———. "Butera: Piano della Fiera, Consi e Fontana Calda," *Mon. Ant.*, vol. XLIV (1958), cols. 205–672.

———. "L'ellenizzazione della Sicilia ed il momento di Ducezio," *Kokalos*, VIII (1962), 167–98.

———. "Le fortificazioni ad aggere nella Sicilia centro-meridionale," *Rend. Acc. Linc.*, ser. VIII, vol. XI (1956), pp. 358–72.

———. "Gibil-Gabib (Caltanissetta). Scavi e ricerche archeologiche," *NSc.*, 1958, pp. 387–408.

———. "Monte Saraceno ed il problema della penetrazione rodio-cretese nella Sicilia meridionale," *Archeol. Class.*, VIII (1956), 121–46.

———. "Note di topografiia siceliota. Parte I," *Kokalos*, IX (1963), 19–48.

———. "Nouvelles fouilles à Géla et dans l'arrière-pays. B: L'arrière-pays (2e partie)," *Rev. Arch.*, XLIX (1957), 147–80.

———. "L'opera di Timoleonte nella Sicilia centro-meridionale vista attraverso gli scavi e le ricerche archeologiche," *Kokalos*, IV (1958), 31–68.

———. "Rapporti tra greci ed indigeni alla luce delle nuove scoperte in Sicilia," *Atti del settimo congresso internazionale di archeologia classica*, 3 vols. (Roma: "L'Erma" di Bretschneider, 1961), vol. II, pp. 45–52.

———. "Scavi e scoperte nella provincia di Caltanisetta dal 1951 al 1957," *NSc.*, 1958, pp. 288–408.

ÅKERSTROM, ÅKE. *Der geometrische Stil in Italien.* [Skrifter utgivna av Svenska institutet i Rom. Ser. I, 4:o. IX (1943).]

ALBRIGHT, WILLIAM FOXWELL. "New Light on the Early History of the Phoenician Colonization," *BASOR*, LXXXIII (1941), 14–22.

ALLEN, HUBERT L. "Excavations at Morgantina (Serra Orlando) 1967–1969. Preliminary Report X," *AJA*, 74 (1970), 359–83.

Das Altertum. Im Auftrage der Sektion für Altertumswissenschaft bei der Deutschen Akademie der Wissenschaften zu Berlin herausgegeben von Johannes Irmscher. Berlin. X (1964).

American Journal of Archaeology. Princeton. 61 (1957), 62 (1958), 64 (1960), 65 (1961), 66 (1962), 68 (1964), 74 (1970).

Ampurias. Revista de arqueología, prehistoria y etnología. Barcelona. XV–XVI (1953–54).

ANDRÉN, ARVID. *Architectural Terracottas from Etrusco-Italic Temples.* Text. [Skrifter utgivna av Svenska institutet i Rom. Ser. I, 4:o. VI (1940).]

The Annual of the British School at Athens. London. LIII–LIV (1958–59).

Annuario della Scuola Archeologica di Atene e delle missioni Italiane in Oriente. Roma. XXVII–XXX (Nuova serie vol. XI–XIII) (1949–51).

Archeologia Classica. Rivista dell'Istituto di archeologia della Università di Roma. Roma. VII (1955)–VIII (1956), XV (1963), XVII (1965), XX (1968).

Archivio storico per la Sicilia Orientale. Catania. Ser. IV, vol. VII (1954).

Archivio storico siracusano. Siracusa. II (1956).

Atti del settimo congresso internazionale di archeologia classica, 3 vols. (Roma: "L'Erma" di Bretschneider, 1961). II.

Atti della (–1946: Reale) Accademia (from 1921:) nazionale dei Lincei. Notizie degli Scavi di Antichità. Roma. 1892, 1899, 1905, 1907, 1920, 1958, 1960, 1967, 1969.

Atti della (–1946: Reale) Accademia (from 1921:) nazionale dei Lincei. Rendiconti. Classe di Scienze morali, storiche e filologiche. Roma. Serie VIII, vol. XII (1957), vol. XVIII (1963).

BECATTI, GIOVANNI. "La leggenda di Dedalo," *Röm. Mitt.,* LX–LXI (1953–54), 22–36.

———. *Oreficerie antiche dalle minoiche alle barbariche* (Roma: Istituto Poligrafico dello Stato, 1955).

BELOCH, JULIUS. "Die Phoeniker am aegaeischen Meer," *Rhein. Mus.,* Neue Folge, XLIX (1894), 111–32.

BÉRARD, JEAN. *La colonisation grecque de l'Italie méridionale et de la Sicile dans l'antiquité: l'histoire et la légende,* 2 éd. (Paris: Presses Universitaires de France, 1957).

BERNABÒ BREA, LUIGI. *Akrai.* Con la collaborazione di Giovanni Pugliese Carratelli e Clelia Laviosa. (Catania, 1956). [Società di Storia Patria per la Sicilia Orientale. Serie III, Monografie Archeologiche della Sicilia. I.]

———. "L'Athenaion di Gela e le sue terrecotte architettoniche," *Annuario Scuola Atene,* XXVII–XXIX (Nuova seria XI–XIII) (1949–51), 7–102.

———. "La Sicilia prehistórica y sus relaciones con Oriente y con la Península Ibérica," *Ampurias,* XV–XVI (1953–54), 137–235.

———. "Leggende e Archeologia nella protostoria Siciliana," *Kokalos,* X–XI (1964–65), Atti del I congresso internazionale di studi sulla Sicilia antica, pp. 1–33.

———. *Sicily before the Greeks* (London: Thames and Hudson, 1957). [Ancient Peoples and Places. 3.]

BERNABÒ BREA, LUIGI, MILITELLO, ELIO, and LA PIANA, SCOLASTICA. "Mineo (Catania). La necropoli detta del Molino della Badia: nuove tombe in contrada Madonna del Piano," *NSc.,* 1969, pp. 210–75.

Bibliothèque des écoles françaises d'Athènes et de Rome. Paris. CLXXXIX (1958).

Bollettino d'arte. Roma. Ser. IV, vol. XLIX (1964).

BOSCH-GIMPERA, PEDRO. "Fragen der Chronologie der phoenizischen Kolonisation in Spanien," *Klio,* XXII (1928), 345–68.

BRELICH, ANGELO. "La religione greca in Sicilia," *Kokalos,* X–XI (1964–65), Atti del I congresso internazionale di studi sulla Sicilia antica, pp. 35–54.

Bulletin de correspondence hellénique. Paris. LXXVI (1952), LXXIX (1955).

Bulletin of the American Schools of Oriental Research, Jerusalem and Baghdad. New Haven, Conn. LXXXIII (1941).

Bullettino di paletnologia italiana. Parma. XVII (1891), XXIII (1897), XXXI (1905).

CARPENTER, RHYS. "A Note on the Foundation Date of Carthage," *AJA,* 68 (1964), 178.

———. "Phoenicians in the West," *AJA,* 62 (1958), 35–53.

CASTAGNOLI, FERDINANDO. *Ippodamo di Mileto e l'urbanistica a pianta ortogonale* (Roma: De Luca editore, 1956).

———. "Recenti ricerche sull' urbanistica ippodamea," *Archeol. Class.,* XV (1963), 180–97.

CATAUDELLA, QUINTINO. "Tragedie di Eschilo nella Siracusa di Gerone," *Kokalos,* X–XI (1964–65), Atti del I congresso internazionale di studi sulla Sicilia antica, pp. 371–98.

CHIAPPISI, STEFANO. *Il Melqart di Sciacca e la questione fenicia in Sicilia* (Roma: Aziende Tip. Eredi G. Bardi, 1961).

CINTAS, PIERRE. "Deux campagnes de fouilles à Utique," *Karthago,* II (1951), 1–88.

———. "Nouvelles recherches à Utique," *Karthago,* V (1954), 89–154.

COOK, JOHN MANUEL. *The Greeks in Ionia and the East* (London: Thames and Hudson, 1962). [Ancient Peoples and Places. 31.]

———. "Old Smyrna," *BSA,* LIII–LIV (1958–59), 1–34.

Cronache di archeologia e di storia dell' arte. Catania. I (1962).

DE MIRO, ERNESTO. *Eraclea Minoa* [breve guida]. (Agrigento: Soprintendenza alle Antichità, 1958).

———. "La fondazione di Agrigento e l'ellenizzazione del territorio fra il Salso e il Platani," *Kokalos,* VIII (1962), 122–52.

———. "Heraclea Minoa. Scavi eseguiti negli anni 1955–56–57," *NSc.,* 1958, pp. 232–87.

———. Il quartiere ellenistico-romano di Agrigento," *Rend. Acc. Linc.,* ser. VIII, vol. XII (1957), 135–40.

DINSMOOR, WILLIAM BELL. *The Architecture of Ancient Greece,* 3d ed., rev. and enl. (London: B. T. Batsford Ltd., 1950).

DI VITA, ANTONINO. "La penetrazione siracusana nella Sicilia sud-orientale alla luce delle più recenti scoperte archeologiche," *Kokalos*, II (1956), 177–205.

———. "Recenti scoperte archeologiche in provincia di Ragusa," *Arch. St. Sir.*, II (1956), 41–44.

DUNBABIN, THOMAS JAMES. "Minos and Daidalos in Sicily," *BSR*, XVI (n.s. III) (1948), 1–18.

———. *The Western Greeks* (Oxford: Clarendon Press, 1948).

EVANS, SIR ARTHUR JOHN. *The Palace of Minos at Knossos*, 4 vols. (London: Macmillan and Co., 1921–36), II:2 (1928), IV:2 (1935).

FALLICO, ANNA MARIA. "Ragusa. Esplorazione di necropoli tarde," *NSc.*, 1967, pp. 407–18.

Festschrift Franz Dornseiff zum 65. Geburtstag. Herausgegeben von Horst Kusch. (Leipzig: VEB Bibliographisches Institut, 1953).

Fontes Hispaniae Antiquae. Auspiciis ac sumptibus Universitatis Litterarum Barcionensis ed. A. Schulten et P. Bosch. (Barcinone [and] Berolini). Fasc. I (1922).

FORRER, EMIL O. "Karthago wurde erst 673–663 v. Chr. gegründet," *Festschrift Franz Dornseiff zum 65. Geburtstag*, pp. 85–93.

Fragmenta Historicorum Graecorum, edd. C. & Th. Mueller, 5 vols. (Paris: Didot, 1841–70). I (1841), II (1848).

FREEMAN, EDWARD AUGUSTUS. *The History of Sicily from the Earliest Times*, 4 vols. (Oxford: Clarendon Press, 1891–94). I (1891), II (1891).

FRÉZOULS, EDMOND. "Une nouvelle hypothèse sur la fondation de Carthage," *BCH*, LXXIX (1955), 155–76.

GALINSKY, G. KARL. *Aeneas, Sicily, and Rome* (Princeton, N.J.: Princeton University Press, 1969).

GARBINI, GIOVANNI. "I Fenici in Occidente," *Studi Etr.*, XXXIV (1966), 111–47.

GIULIANO, ANTONIO. *Urbanistica delle città greche* (Milano: Il Saggiatore, 1966).

GJERSTAD, EINAR. See *The Swedish Cyprus Expedition*.

GRIFFO, PIETRO. "Sull' identificazione di Camico con l'odierna S. Angelo Muxaro a nord-ovest di Agrigento," *Arch. Stor. Sic. Orient.*, ser. 4, vol. VII (1954), fasc. I–III, pp. 58–78.

GRIFFO, PIETRO, and VON MATT, LEONARD. *Gela, The Ancient Greeks in Sicily* (New York: New York Graphic Society, Ltd.; printed in Italy by AGIS-Stringa, Genoa, 1968).

HARDEN, DONALD BENJAMIN. *The Phoenicians* (London: Thames and Hudson, 1962). [Ancient Peoples and Places. 26.]

HERACLEIDES PONTICUS. "Fragmenta," *FHG*, II (1848).

Hesperia. Athens. XII (1943).

HILL, SIR GEORGE FRANCIS. *Catalogue of the Greek Coins of Cyprus* (London: British Museum–Department of Coins and Medals, 1904). [A Catalogue of the Greek Coins in the British Museum. 24.]

Historia. Zeitschrift für alte Geschichte. Wiesbaden. IX (1960).

Inscriptiones Graecae. Consilio et auctoritate Academiae Litterarum Borussicae editae. (Ed. minor; Berolini apud Gualterum de Gruyter et socios). I (. . . ed. Fridericus Hiller de Gaertringen, 1924).

Karthago. Revue trimestrielle d'archéologie africaine. Paris. II (1951), V (1954).

Klio. Beiträge zur alten Geschichte. Leipzig. XXII (Neue Folge IV) (1928).

Kokalos Κώκαλος. Studi pubblicati dall'Istituto di Storia Antica dell'Università di Palermo. Palermo. II (1956), III (1957), IV (1958), VIII (1962), IX (1963), X–XI (1964–65).

MANNI, EUGENIO. "Minosse ed Eracle nella Sicilia dell'età del bronzo," *Kokalos*, VIII (1962), 6–29.

———. *Sicilia pagana* (Palermo: S. F. Flaccovio, 1963).

MATT, LEONARD VON. See Griffo, Pietro, *Gela*.

Mitteilungen des Deutschen Archäologischen Instituts. Römische Abteilung. Rom; Heidelberg. XIII (1898), XXIV (1909), LX–LXI (1953–54), LXVI (1959).

Monumenti antichi. Pubblicati per cura della (–1946: Reale) Accademia (from 1921:) Nazionale dei Lincei. Milano., Roma. II (1893). VI (1895), VII (1897), XVIII (1908), XX (1911), XLIV (1958), XLVII (1966).

MOSCATI, SABATINO, "La questione fenicia," *Rend. Acc. Linc.*, ser. VIII, vol. XVIII (1963), 483–506.

———. *The World of the Phoenicians* (London: Weidenfeld and Nicolson, 1968).

NILSSON, MARTIN. P. *Geschichte der griechischen Religion*, I (3., durchgesehene und ergänzte Auflage; München: C. H. Beck'sche Verlagsbuchhandlung, 1967). [Handbuch der Altertumswissenschaft. A. V:2.1.]

———. *The Mycenaean Origin of Greek Mythology* (New York: The Norton Library, 1963).

NYLANDER, CARL. "Remarks on the Urartian Acropolis at Zernaki Tepe," *Orientalia Suecana*, XIV–XV (1965–66), 141–54.

Opuscula Archaeologica. II (1941). See Skrifter utgivna av Svenska Institutet i Rom. Ser. I. 4:o. Vol. V.

Opuscula Romana. IV (1962), VI (1968). See Skrifter utgivna av Svenska Institutet i Rom. Ser. I. 4:o. Vols. XXII and XXIX.

Orientalia Suecana. Edenda curavit Frithiof Rundgren. Stockholm. XIV–XV (1965–66).

ORLANDINI, PIERO. "Arte indigena e colonizzazione greca in Sicilia," *Kokalos*, X–XI (1964–65), Atti del I congresso internazionale di studi sulla Sicilia antica, pp. 539–44.

ORLANDINI, PIERO. "Arule arcaiche a rilievo nel Museo Nazionale di Gela," *Röm. Mitt.*, LXVI (1959), 97–103.

———. "L'espansione di Gela nella Sicilia centromeridionale," *Kokalos*, VIII (1962), 69–121.

———. "Sabucina. A) Scoperte varie. B) Prima campagna di scavo (1962). Rapporto preliminare," *Archeol. Class.*, XV (1963), 86–96.

———. "Sabucina. La seconda campagna di scavo (1964). Rapporto preliminare," *Archeol. Class.*, XVII (1965), 133–40.

———. "Sabucina: la terza campagna di scavo (1966). Rapporto preliminare," *Archeol. Class.*, XX (1968), 151–56.

ORSI, PAOLO. "Anathemata di una città siculo-greca a Terravecchia di Grammichele (Catania)," *Mon. Ant.*, vol. XVIII (1908), cols. 121–68.

———. "Di una anonima città siculo-greca a Monte S. Mauro presso Caltagirone (scavi dal 1903 al 1905)," *Mon. Ant.*, vol. XX (1911), cols. 729–850.

———. "D'una città greca a Terravecchia presso Grammichele in provincia di Catania," *Mon. Ant.*, vol. VII (1897), cols. 201–74.

———. "Fittili con un verso del comico Frinico e scoperte varie," *NSc.*, 1920, pp. 336–37.

———. "M. Bubbonia (Comune di Mazzarino)," *NSc.*, 1907, pp. 497–98.

———. "M. Bubbonia (Comune di Mazzarino). Città e necropoli sicula dei tempi greci," *NSc.*, 1905, pp. 447–49.

———. "Le necropoli di Licodia Eubea ed i vasi geometrici del quarto periodo siculo," *Röm. Mitt.*, XIII (1898), 305–66.

———. "Necropoli e stazioni sicule di transizione. V. Necropoli al Molino della Badia presso Grammichele," *BPI*, XXXI (1905), 96–133.

———. "La necropoli sicula del Plemmirio (Siracusa)," *BPI*, XVII (1891), 115–39.

———. "Necropoli sicula presso Siracusa con vasi e bronzi micenei," *Mon. Ant.*, vol. II (1893), cols. 5–36.

———. "Ragusa. Nuove esplorazioni nella necropoli di Hybla Heraea," *NSc.*, 1899, pp. 402–18.

———. "Ragusa (῞Υβλα ῾Ηραία). Di alcuni sepolcri spettanti all'arcaica necropoli e di altre minori scoperte," *NSc.*, 1892, pp. 321–32.

———. "Sepolcri di transizione dalla civiltà sicula alla greca. I. Ipogeo siculo grecizzante di Licodia Eubea," *Röm. Mitt.*, XXIV (1909), 59–73.

———. "Thapsos," *Mon. Ant.*, vol. VI (1895), cols. 89–150.

ORSI, PAOLO, et al. "Eloro," *Mon. Ant.*, vol. XLVII (1966), cols. 203–340.

PACE, BIAGIO. *Arte e civiltà della Sicilia antica*, 4 vols. (Milano: Società anonima editrice Dante Alighieri, [Albrighi Segati & C.], 1935–49). I (1935).

PAIS, ETTORE. *Storia della Sicilia e della Magna Grecia* (Torino, 1894).

Papers and Monographs of the American Academy in Rome. Rome. XIV (1952).

Papers of the British School at Rome. London. XVI (n.s. III) (1948).

PARETI, LUIGI. *Sicilia antica* (Palermo: Palumbo, 1959).

Paulys Read-Encyclopädie der classischen Altertumswissenschaft. Neue Bearbeitung. Begonnen von Georg Wissowa . . . (Stuttgart: J. B. Metzlersche Verlagsbuchhandlung). XV (1932).

PELAGATTI, PAOLA. "Naxos—relazione preliminare delle campagne di scavo 1961–64," *Bd'A*, 1964, pp. 149–65.

PHILISTUS. "Fragmenta," *FHG*, I (1841).

PIRAINO, MARIA TERESA. "Sulla cronologia delle fondazioni sceliote," *Kokalos*, III (1957), 123–28.

PUGLIESE CARRATELLI, GIOVANNI. "Minos e Cocalos," *Kokalos*, II (1956), 89–103.

RAUBITSCHEK, A. E. "Greek Inscriptions," *Hesp.*, XII (1943), 12–88.

Revue archéologique. Paris. XLIX (1957).

Rheinisches Museum für Philologie. Frankfurt am Main. Neue Folge, XLIX (1894).

RICHTER, GISELA M. A. *Kouroi. Archaic Greek Youths* (London: The Phaidon Press, 1960).

RIZZA, GIOVANNI. "Siculi e greci sui colli di Leontini," *Cronache di archeologia e di storia dell'arte*, I (1962), 3–27.

SCHENK VON STAUFFENBERG, ALEXANDER. "Dorieus," *Historia*, IX (1960), 181–215.

———. *Trinakria.* Sizilien und Grossgriechenland in archaischer und frühklassischer Zeit (Wien: R. Oldenbourg Verlag, 1963).

SCHIFMAN, ILJA. "Die phönikische Kolonisation des westlichen Mittelmeeres" [Deutsche Übersetzung von Ulf Lehman], *Das Altertum*, X (1964), 195–201.

SCHMIEDT, GIULIO. "Applicazioni della fotografia aerea in ricerche estensive di topografia antica in Sicilia," *Kokalos*, III (1957), 18–30.

SCHMIEDT, GIULIO, and GRIFFO, PIETRO. *Agrigento antica dalle fotografie aeree e dai recenti scavi* ([Estratto da L'Universo. Anno XXXVIII (1958)]; Firenze: Istituto Geografico Militare, 1958).

SHOE, LUCY TAXIS. *Profiles of Western Greek Mouldings.* [Papers and Monographs of the American Academy in Rome. XIV (1952).]

SJÖQVIST, ERIK. "Excavations at Morgantina (Serra Orlando) 1959. Preliminary Report IV," *AJA*, 64 (1960), 125–35.

———. "Excavations at Morgantina (Serra Orlando) 1961. Preliminary Report VI," *AJA*, 66 (1962), 135–43.

———. "Excavations at Morgantina (Serra Orlando) 1963. Preliminary Report VIII," *AJA*, 68 (1964), 137–47.

———. "Excavations at Serra Orlando (Morgantina). Preliminary Report II," *AJA*, 62 (1958), 155–62.

———. "I greci a Morgantina," *Kokalos*, VIII (1962), 52–68.

———. "Heracles in Sicily," *Opusc. Rom.*, IV (1962), 117–23.

———. "Timoleonte e Morgantina," *Kokalos*, IV (1958), 107–18.

Skrifter utgivna av Svenska institutet i Rom. Acta Instituti Romani regni Sueciae. Lund. Ser. I. 4:0. V (1941), VI (1940), IX (1943), XXII (1962), XXIX (1968).

STILLWELL, RICHARD. "Excavations at Morgantina (Serra Orlando) 1960. Preliminary Report V," *AJA*, 65 (1961), 277–81.

———. "Excavations at Morgantina (Serra Orlando) 1962. Preliminary Report VII," *AJA*, 67 (1963), 163–71.

Studi Annibalici. Atti del convegno svoltosi a Cortona—Tuoro sul Trasimeno—Perugia ottobre 1961 ([Estratto da Accademia Crusca—Cortona. Annuario XII, n.s. V (1961–64)]; Cortona: Tipografia Commerciale, 1964).

Studi etruschi. Firenze. XXXIV (1966).

The Swedish Cyprus Expedition. Finds and Results of the Excavations in Cyprus 1927–1931. Vol. IV, pt. II. The Cypro-Geometric, Cypro-Archaic, and Cypro-Classical Periods, by Einar Gjerstad. (Stockholm: The Swedish Cyprus Expedition [Vitterhetsakademien], 1948).

SÄFLUND, GÖSTA. "Ionisches und Dorisches in Magna Graecia," *Opuscula Archaeologica*, II (1941) [=Skrifter utgivna av Svenska institutet i Rom. Ser. I, 4:0. Vol. V (1941)], 77–91.

TAYLOUR, LORD WILLIAM. *Mycenaean Pottery in Italy and Adjacent Areas* (Cambridge: at the University Press, 1958). [Occasional Publications of the Cambridge University Museum of Archaeology and Ethnology. V.]

TUSA, VINCENZO. "La questione fenicio-punica in Sicilia," *Studi Annibalici*, pp. 37–55.

VALLET, GEORGES. "La colonisation chalcidienne et l'hellénisation de la Sicile orientale," *Kokalos*, VIII (1962), 30–51.

———. *Rhégion et Zancle.* Histoire, commerce et civilisation des cités chalcidiennes du détroit de Messine (Paris: E. de Boccard, 1958). [Bibliothèque des Écoles françaises d'Athènes et de Rome. CLXXXIX.]

VALLET, GEORGES, and VILLARD, FRANCOIS. "Les dates de fondation de Megara Hyblaea et de Syracuse," *BCH*, LXXVI (1952), 289–346.

WARMINGTON, BRIAN HERBERT. *Carthage* (London: Robert Hale Limited, 1960).

WENTKER, HERMANN. *Sizilien und Athen* (Heidelberg: Quelle & Meyer, 1956).

Index

Number in italics refer to pages with illustrations.